Good in
Every Thing

GOOD IN EVERY THING

Meditations on Shakespeare

JOSH MAYO

CiRCE
Concord, NC

Published in the USA
by the CiRCE Institute
© 2021 by Joshua Mayo

ISBN: 978-1-7347853-5-7

All rights reserved. This publication may not be reproduced, stored in a retireval system, or transmitted, in any form, or by any means, without the prior written permission of the CiRCE Institute.

For information:
CiRCE Institute
81 McCachern Blvd
Concord, NC 28025

Cover design by Graeme Pitman
Layout by Goldberry Studios

Printed in the United States of America.

For Bethany

CONTENTS

Introduction 1

CHAPTER ONE - 5
Hamlet & What Moves Us

CHAPTER TWO - 13
Three Unoffensive Themes in *The Taming of the Shrew*

CHAPTER THREE - 33
A Thousand Several Tongues: Conscience in *Richard III*

CHAPTER FOUR - 39
The Converse of Breath in *Love's Labour's Lost*

CHAPTER FIVE - 47
Midsummer: A Case Study in Poetic Imagination

CHAPTER SIX - 55
Henry V and the Shrugging Shakespeare

CHAPTER SEVEN - 63
The Wonder of Arden

CHAPTER EIGHT - 77
How Could Brutus Love Caesar?

CHAPTER NINE - 83
The Tempest and the Limits of Literature

APPENDIX - 91
Five Strategies for Sticking with Shakespeare

Notes - 99

And this our life, exempt from public haunt,
Finds tongues in trees, books in the running brooks,
Sermons in stones, and good in every thing.

—As You Like It
Act II, Scene I

INTRODUCTION

The learner must want to be changed by his studies.
He must read Shakespeare as a Christian reads his Bible.

David V. Hicks, *Norms & Nobility*

This little book offers a handful of reflections touching on some of Shakespeare's plays that have brought me a precious supply of refreshment and joy over the years. The term "meditations" in the title may conjure up a host of strange and eclectic associations: anything from stoicism to jazz music to lavender-scented yoga pillows. But I think the practice I have in mind is something fairly familiar and intuitive for readers (though, sadly, it is too little exercised). In the following pages, we will pursue the simple pleasure of thinking with Shakespeare—by which we mean a different thing than the ordinary academic enterprise of thinking about Shakespeare. Today our shelves teem with criticisms, commentaries, histories, and variorums, many of which are vitally helpful, even needful, to understanding and appreciating the Bard's classic body of work. But in these nine short reflections, I want to try out a different way of appreciating literature that has its roots in a rich history of Christian and classical thought: something the old grammarians used to call *meditatio*—our natural, imaginative desire to look at important life questions through the eyes of a beloved author.

The historicist impulse of modern education tends to treat literature as an artifact. Many critics and teachers think of books primarily as literary relics that tell us something about the time and place of the author, but very little about our own condition, much less about those higher-order questions that loom over our personal lives. The Great Tradition thought otherwise. St. Basil of Caesarea believed that even pagan literature was a source of divine truth,[1] and John Calvin called the classics "admirable light" that illumines our souls.[2] David Hicks speaks for the broad classical consensus when he insists that we "must read Shakespeare as a Christian reads his Bible."[3] Not that Shakespeare could ever become a kind of dramatic Scripture or poetic Bible-substitute. But Bible-reading and Shakespeare-reading ought to share a common hope which the modern critic often lacks: the sincere expectation that one can learn something important about life through the printed page.

The practice of literary meditation has been around for a long time. In his *Didascalicon*, the twelfth-century theologian Hugh of St. Victor explains the crucial qualitative difference between reading for "understanding" and reading for "counsel." Whereas *studio* typically happens along systematic lines (the analysis of a plot, the scrutiny of an argument), *meditatio* transpires through any of the numerous and sometimes haphazard ways that a book can spark a flame in our souls. The art of meditation, Victor says,

> *delights to range along open ground, where it fixes its free gaze upon the contemplation of truth, drawing together now these, now those causes of things, or now penetrating into profundities, leaving nothing doubtful, nothing obscure. The start of learning, thus, lies in reading, but its consummation lies in meditation.*[4]

Clearly, there isn't a single method to be followed in this description, but an overarching commitment to wisdom in contemplation. The spirit of meditation, not the system, proves to be the vital thing. All literary learning begins in study, but at some point we must attend to those scenes and speeches in Shakespeare that jump out at us. In Francis Bacon's phrase, we must "weigh and consider" what the text is telling us.[5] This kind of imaginative reception isn't something separate from serious reading. It is the "consummation" of all our efforts.

There is no single, continuous argument to this book. The reflections that follow are episodic, and that means there is a degree of arbitrariness both in the choice of plays and in the topics they inspire. Still, these chapters generally cohere around the subjects of education, imagination, and virtue: the paideia of the soul, the expansive vision of the heart, and the ideals of human excellence. My intended audience is someone who knows a little Shakespeare, cares about classical stuff, and doesn't mind hearing some thoughts on the latter suggested by the former.

The practice of meditating on Shakespeare turns out to have a long and (mostly) venerable history. Abraham Lincoln made a habit of always keeping a thumb in a volume of Shakespeare. As did John Keats. And the illustrious P. G. Wodehouse. But no one I think surpasses the fervor of Coleridge, who was perhaps the most enthusiastic supporter of a regular Shakespeare reading-plan:

> *O! When I think of the inexhaustible mine of virgin treasure in our Shakespeare, that I have been almost daily reading him since I was ten years old . . . that at every new accession of information, after every successful exercise of meditation, and every fresh presentation of experience, I have unfailingly discovered a proportionate increase of wisdom and intuition in Shakespeare.*[6]

Maybe I should end there and issue this outrageous invitation as my own. Don't just read Shakespeare—read him with the expectation that you will be changed by him. These plays are a quarry for the conscience and a storehouse for high ideas. Read him as though he has something illuminating and personal to say to you. Because he does.

CHAPTER ONE

HAMLET & WHAT MOVES US

By our efforts to bring together and to understand the conflicts from within that are engendered by images of conflicts from without, somehow, miraculously, we learn.

Louise Cowan, "The Literary Mode of Knowing"

If Polonius were a professor, he would almost certainly wear tweed—a medium gray weave, knit elbow patches, and a smart opal pocket square (folded to a single peak, of course). If Polonius were a don, he would likely own Gregory Peck frames: the classic tortoiseshell type with a lightweight build. A collegiate Polonius would probably devise ripping PowerPoints, replete with fully documented images and animating spiral text. He'd probably subscribe to all the trending journals, mill about at conferences, and drop buzzwords like "high-impact practices" and "diagnostic teaching" with a smidge of impish glee. In short, if Polonius were a professor, he would be very professorial. But I am not sure that he would be a very good professor.

From the start, Hamlet's relationship with this tiresome court counselor is a vexed one. First, Polonius serves Claudius, the devious uncle who murdered Hamlet's father to gain the crown. Second, he is the father of Ophelia, Hamlet's love interest in a "complicated relationship" to end all complicated relationships. Additionally, though, the situation is vexed by a contrast of personalities. Really, there could hardly be two men less similar than Hamlet and Polonius.

When it comes to public polish, Polonius boasts an undeniable degree of *savoir faire*, but when it comes to public influence, Shakespeare's "tedious old fool" is a bit of a bore (2.2.219). Wordy, ostentatious, dull—Polonius possesses a capacity for circumlocution which far exceeds his circumspection. Recall, for example, this memorable string of proverbs (delivered with all the delicacy and grace of a T-shirt cannon) just before his son, Laertes, skips off to France:

> *Give every man thy ear but few thy voice;*
> *Take each man's censure but reserve thy judgment.*
> *Costly thy habit as thy purse can buy*
> *But not expressed in fancy—rich, not gaudy . . .*
> *Neither a borrower nor a lender, be,*
> *For loan oft loses both itself and friend*
> *And borrowing dulleth th' edge of husbandry.*
> *This above all, to thine own self be true*
> *And it must follow as the night the day*
> *Thou canst not then be false*
>   *to any man.* (1.3.67–70, 74–79)

Put a pin in that last piece of suspicious advice for a moment. Has this kind of moral teaching worked on Laertes? Polonius' suspicion is telling. Anticipating those "wanton, wild, and usual slips / As are companions noted and most known / To youth and liberty," a very dubious dad sends his servant Reynaldo on a reconnaissance mission to Paris to check up on his son's activities (2.1.22–24). Ophelia too begs her brother not to act like the "puff'd and reckless libertine" who sallies down "the primrose path of dalliance" (1.3.49–50). In manners, Laertes possesses *sprezzatura*—spontaneous grace. The courtier Osric describes him as "an absolute gentleman, full of most excellent differences, of very soft society, and great showing" (5.2.106–8). Yet when it comes to character, Laertes' education seems partial at best.

I do not think Shakespeare means to cast doubt on moral exhortation itself. Nor do I think he has a problem with proverbial wisdom. If you nix the proverb genre, then you have to throw out, well, Proverbs—not to mention a whole stash of other gems, like *The Golden Sayings of Epictetus* (something an Elizabethan literary-type would certainly never do). The real issue seems instead to be a life in which style is shorn of wisdom. Polonius is the kind of person who memorizes sayings not because he is wise (or hopes to become wise), but because he aims at "soft society." No wonder Laertes follows suit. Like father, like son (proverbially speaking).

Here is another counterfactual: If Prince Hamlet turned teacher, what would he be like? Would he pair a black turtleneck with a black blazer? Would he lecture like Jacques

Lacan, pacing the room in saturnine steps, waving his Lucky Strike cigarette with great panache? I am more reluctant to speak on this point because Hamlet is a much deeper character than Polonius, and for that reason, who can say what Hamlet would or wouldn't do? Still, I suspect the prince understands something vitally important that Polonius totally misses: the art of what really moves people.

Remember act 2, scene 2—the scene where Hamlet greets the players at Elsinore? Hamlet requests an impromptu performance of Virgil, specifically the scene of Priam's death at the fall of Troy. During the vivid spectacle that follows, Polonius shows only mild interest ("This is too long," he mutters baldly at one point), but by contrast, Hamlet is visibly moved (2.2.498). The prince has "turn'd his color and / has tears in's eyes" (2.2.519–520). Only in a lengthy soliloquy that closes the act does Hamlet personally divulge the matter of his discomposure:

> *O, what a rogue and peasant slave am I!*
> *Is it not monstrous that this player here,*
> *But in a fiction, in a dream of passion,*
> *Could force his soul so to his own conceit*
> *That from her working all his visage wann'd,*
> *Tears in his eyes, distraction in his aspect,*
> *A broken voice, an' his whole function suiting*
> *With forms to his conceit? And all for nothing,*
> *For Hecuba!*
> *What's Hecuba to him, or he to Hecuba,*

> *That he should weep for her? What would he do*
> *Had he the motive and the cue for passion*
> *That I have? (2.2.550–62)*

In a flash, Shakespeare's audience grasps something about the power of imagination as a conduit of moral feeling. Priam's wife Hecuba may mean nothing to this professional thespian, but she certainly means something to Hamlet, who glimpses in her character a devastating reminder of his mother's infidelity. In a sudden moment of poetic apprehension, Queen Hecuba stands for the kind of queen Gertrude ought to be, and even Hamlet feels some chastisement from this classic image of loyalty (2.2.502). So something strange and powerful transpires. Engaging the story of Priam as his own story, Hamlet discovers a living relationship with the contemplated object. He is moved.

Anyone who has deeply loved stories recognizes what is happening here. If you have read *The Divine Comedy* or *The Brothers Karamazov* or *Barchester Towers*, you know how poetic images help us see the beauty of beauty and the evil of evil and the silliness of silliness. In Hamlet's own words to the players, these imaginative pictures raise "the mirror up to nature, to show virtue her own feature, scorn her own image" (3.2.22–23). Hamlet clearly apprehends the inner pedagogical principle at play, because he immediately plans to wield its power against Claudius:

> *I'll have these players*
> *Play something like the murder of my father*
> *Before mine uncle. I'll observe his looks;*
> *I'll tent him to the quick: if he but blench,*
> *I know my course. (3.3.590–94)*

With this "Mousetrap," the prince creates the conditions for the stage to do the same work on Claudius (3.2.237). He stages a play containing a murder scene eerily similar to the deed suspected of his uncle, and he hopes by this device to call out the pangs of hidden guilt: "The play's the thing" to "catch the conscience of the king" (2.2.604–5). What is more, the plan works. Seeing his own evil on display, Claudius is cut to the quick, just as Hamlet was by Hecuba. Gonzago's audience does not know why Claudius loses his composure, but Hamlet's audience does: Dramatic confirmation arrives in act three, scene three when we find a guilt stricken sovereign soliloquizing a confession: "My offense is rank, it smells to heaven." The king is moved.

So why does Hamlet's pedagogy move the soul while Polonius' doesn't? To put not too fine a point on it, the fundamental contrast between Hamlet's "education" and Polonius' is that the former is poetic in nature: Hamlet discovers a moral feeling by seeing that moral feeling enacted. In the case of Laertes, we have a young man who is told what the good life looks like. In the case of the prince, by contrast, we have a soul who is shown it. The difference, again, is not with the medium, not between plays and proverbs (for proverbs have always been used to express vital truths). The difference is rather between truth encountered didactically and truth encountered experientially. Polonius may know all the watchwords of courtly life, but only Hamlet watches.

The great poets teach us that to truly learn something, to apprehend a reality with the whole of our being, we must not merely be told about it; we must, like Hamlet, see reality for ourselves. Here "seeing" means the whole sensorium and not just the ocular sense. With the help of the whole body, the soul directly beholds the reality at hand, contemplates it, and takes it in, and we call this event *poetica scientia*—that luminescent moment in which, John Senior explains, "we intuitively know that something is due to our experience of being."[1]

Of course, *poetica scientia*, also known as poetic knowledge, is not limited to the study of poetry. A little boy wrestles with his dog and recognizes the goodness of dog-ness. A botany student encounters the wild outline of a white oak and perceives the beauty of nature's forms. A Danish prince watches an actor and weeps over his life. So on and so on. This is an idea for teachers to take to the bank. Deep education, learning by looking, drops its taproot into the soil of the soul and turns the mind to the essences of things—trees, songs, heroes, chemicals, theorems—so we can see their nature firsthand. Perhaps this is what the great Charlotte Mason meant when she insisted that all genuine education must be "literary"—not that all learning should take place in the form of verse, but that all learning must possess the poetic soul which causes a student to see.²

Polonius may not have worn tweed, and he may not have shopped at Oliver Peoples. Still, it is too bad that he cared more about the stylish catchphrases of courtiers than the precious, unmediated glimpse of wisdom. For as Josef Pieper so brilliantly observes, "In seeing for ourselves, we are achieving more contact with reality and are in greater possession of reality than when we espouse knowledge based on hearing."³ At the end of the day, our deepest moral affections belong to the world of the spiritual sight.

CHAPTER TWO

THREE UNOFFENSIVE THEMES IN THE TAMING OF THE SHREW

. . . primitive, somewhat brutal stuff.

Sir Arthur Quiller-Couch

"*Taming of the Shrew*" lectures the poet W. H. Auden late in 1946, "is the only play of Shakespeare's that is a complete failure, though *Titus Andronicus* may be another." The central characters are a flop, he argues: Petruchio is a "cad," and Katherina disappoints us with her "failure to protest successfully." Farce, by its very nature, makes light of things, and misogyny is one of those things we shouldn't take lightly. Here the poet downshifts from critical to cool, breathing out sangfroid like the blue smoke from one of his iconic cigarettes: "The play's a bore."[1]

Shrew is full of ambiguous bits, so we understand why some read this play as a story of cruelty and control—in one writer's description, "the *idée fixé* that a man must command absolute obedience from his wife."[2] Is it possible that behind the cheery, chirpy conventions of farce lies a truly terrible *dénouement*? As Anne Barton has observed, "No other play by Shakespeare depends so heavily upon theatrical realization as opposed to mere reading."[3]

Woe betide the man who disagrees with Auden. Still, his blanket belief that "Shakespeare is not a writer of farce" may do injustice to the playwright's amazing ability to reinvent genres for his own poetic purposes.[4] Sure, the play follows some of the standard conventions of farce (humorous disguises, slapstick beatings, outrageous banter, etc.). But I think that Shakespeare's play has a higher aim than slapdash sexism. Without ignoring the squeamish bits, we might consider three higher themes that emerge throughout *The Taming of the Shrew*. Auden may be right about farce in general, but in *The Shrew* we find something more substantial: in Russell Fraser's words, "something deeper and more permanent than the mode."[5]

Theme #1: The Passions Pose a Human Problem

Shrew's induction provides a hint that the play is more than a battle of the sexes. Before we meet the main shrew character, Katherina, we meet another shrew character—one that happens to be (surprise!) a man. In Shakespeare's curious frame-story, a drunken tinker named Sly breaks a glass at the local tavern and refuses to pay the hostess for the loss on the grounds of his supposed pedigree: "Y' are a baggage, the Slys are no rogues. Look in the chronicles; we came in with Richard Conqueror" (Prologue.1.3–5). Sly falls asleep, and a passing Lord conscripts his servants, fellow hunters, and a

3 UNOFFENSIVE THEMES IN *THE TAMING OF THE SHREW*

troupe of players in a prank on him:

What think you, if he were convey'd to bed,
Wrapp'd in sweet clothes, rings put upon his fingers,
　A most delicious banquet by his bed,
　　And brave attendants near him when he wakes,
　　　Would not the beggar then forget himself?
(Prologue.1.37–41)

They take the sozzled tinker to one of the Lord's rooms and decorate the space with lascivious pictures of Io and Daphne, readying the room with musicians, strewn flowers, and waiting attendants. In the most elaborate part of the plan, the Lord's page Bartholomew dresses like a noblewoman to play the part of Sly's wife, now elated by the sudden recovery of her husband. Awaking, the once self-promoting Sly stares in disbelief at the scene which greets him: "Am not I Christopher Sly, old Sly's son of Burton-heath, by birth a pedlar, by education a card-maker, by transmutation a bear-herd, and now by present profession a tinker?" (Prologue.2.17–21). The Lord and servants call Sly's attention to the lifelike images of lust and promise him that he "hast a lady far more beautiful / Than any woman in this waning age," a wife "inferior to none" (Prologue.62–63, 67). Sly believes the ploy and for the first time speaks in blank verse:

Am I a lord, and have I such a lady?
　Or do I dream? Or have I dream'd till now?

> *I do not sleep: I see, I hear, I speak;*
> *I smell sweet savors, and I feel soft things.*
> *Upon my life, I am a lord indeed,*
> *And not a tinker, nor Christopher Sly. (Prologue.68–73)*

Presently, Bartholomew emerges to play the part of the doting and obedient wife. But when Sly gets amorous, the page restrains the tinker's passions with doctor's orders. The players promise to distract him with a "pleasant comedy," and thus begins our story of Kate and Petruchio, a play-within-the-play (Prologue.130).

Incidentally, apart from one brief moment at the end of act one, scene one, *Shrew* does not return to the frame-story, though some scholars believe that the play originally contained an epilogue that circled back to the curious predicament of Christopher Sly. This textual question is interesting, but the more important matter for our purposes is the theme established by the frame: the transformation of unruly passions. Sly anticipates Kate as a male example of this theme, and the clarity of this parallel across the sexes with its decidedly egalitarian spin on the traditional shrew tale invites the audience to broaden its conception of shrewishness beyond the quarrelsome termagant. Shakespeare, it seems, pushes the boundaries of the shrew tale to get at something more universal and less gender-specific: not the shrewish she, but the shrewish soul.

3 UNOFFENSIVE THEMES IN *THE TAMING OF THE SHREW*

Theme #2: Reason Alone Is a Bad Chaperone for the Passions

Once we grant this initial idea—this first intuition that Shakespeare's play not only considers the turbulence of male–female relationships, but also the larger moral question of how we tame our unruly passions—we begin to grasp the import of various subplots in the play and understand how seemingly minor episodes prove vital to the larger theme of desire. Not just Kate, but many characters find themselves drawn hither and thither by runaway passions, and the attentive audience must observe these characters' choices and judge them according to their fruits. We must ask: What kind of soul is susceptible to disordered desire? What kind of soul stands strong?

By the end of the first scene, we know what doesn't work: the purely rational approach to governing our passions. This fact becomes obvious right at the beginning of Shakespeare's play, when characters who are otherwise very intelligent soon become very silly. The action opens in the streets of Padua, where Lucentio, the son of the rich merchant, and Tranio, his wily servant, are hashing out a plan for their time at University. Lucentio aspires to study virtue and "suck the sweets of sweet philosophy," but Tranio warns him against taking too strict a design for his studies:

> *While we do admire*
> *This virtue and this moral discipline,*

> *Let's be no Stoics nor no stocks, I pray,*
> *Or so devote to Aristotle's checks*
> *As Ovid be an outcast quite abjur'd.*
> *Balk logic with acquaintance that you have,*
> *And practice rhetoric in your common talk,*
> *Music and poesy use to quicken you,*
> *The mathematics, and the metaphysics,*
> *Fall to them as you find your stomach serves you;*
> *No profit grows where no pleasure ta'en.*
> *In brief, sir, study what you most affect. (1.1.29–40)*

No right-thinking person would deny that desire plays an important role in the process of education. The student's affections must be engaged for true learning to take place. But is this haphazard curriculum good advice? Should Lucentio allow his appetite, his "affect," to dictate his pursuits? Learning with desire and learning according to one's desires are two radically different things. In the former situation, reason governs, and the will motivates. But in the latter, reason follows the lead of the passions. Unfortunately, Lucentio embraces Tranio's open curriculum model, a choice that threatens trouble even in the very same scene. The next sequence that unfolds presents a funny picture of what happens when the "stomach" takes over the mind, as Lucentio very quickly goes from being an eager student of virtue to a hopeless slave of desire.

Presently, a Paduan gentleman named Baptista enters with his daughters, Katherina and Bianca, and Bianca's two suit-

3 UNOFFENSIVE THEMES IN *THE TAMING OF THE SHREW*

ors, Gremio and Hortensio, and it's clear in this moment that an agitation has erupted around the two girls. Both Gremio and Hortensio are vying for Bianca, but Baptista refuses to release her in marriage until he has first found a spouse for Katherina, a lady who at present is in no mood for matrimony. Things grow tense. Hortensio chides Kate for not being of a nicer disposition, and Kate in turn threatens "to comb" Hortensio's "noddle with a three-legged stool" (1.1.69, 64). Sensing this as a good exit moment, Bianca excuses herself to some unfinished schoolwork ("books and instruments shall be my company"), and the studiously-minded Lucentio is smitten:

> ... now in plainness do confess to thee [Tranio],
> That are to me as secret and as dear
> As Anna to the Queen of Carthage was:
> Tranio, I burn, I pine, I perish, Tranio,
> If I achieve not this young modest girl. (1.1.82–83, 152–56)

So much for the philosopher. With this melodramatic, muddled allusion to Virgil's *Aeneid*, reason runs out the door even before the end of act 1, scene 1. In Lucentio's mixed-up analogy, Tranio is Anna, Bianca is Aeneas, and Lucentio himself is the pining, perishing Dido: The servant turns sister, the lady turns knight, and the suitor plays the role of the languishing wife. Obviously, Lucentio's passions have unmoored him. He is caught by "love in idleness" (151).

Such a quick capitulation to feeling demonstrates the tenuous relationship between what the mind believes and the appetite craves: Reason alone proves a bad chaperone to the passions. Lucentio's head by itself cannot rule his belly.

Theme #3: Imagination Informs Right Action

In the classical framework of virtue formation, the mind must govern the passions through the imagining-valuing-willing core of the human, for if the heart fails to purify the passions by mediating knowledge to desire, the mind caves to the appetites every time.[6] Instead of the head ruling the belly, the belly rules the head, just as we saw with Lucentio. But when the soul harnesses desire to reason by means of the will, it stands fortified against the base drives of whim. This imaginative approach to virtue is precisely what we find in Petruchio, who attempts to curb Kate's passions just as the trickster Lord and his men tamed Christopher Sly's in the induction: through the power of images. The soul needs a healthy imagination to arbitrate the competing demands of the mind and the appetites, so it is no surprise that Petruchio targets this faculty in Kate through his wild and wacky theatricality.

Enter the plucky Veronese gentleman who plans to win the heart of Katherina and thereby bring about the comic conclusion for all parties. How exactly does Petruchio set out to woo Kate? How does he aim to entice her passions? Strangely enough, through imagination and performance. By acting in various roles, Petruchio reveals things to Kate about herself—both who she is in her disposition and to whom she might

3 UNOFFENSIVE THEMES IN *THE TAMING OF THE SHREW*

be transformed. Principally, this task involves two strategies. In the first, he teases Kate with an image of a reformed self, praising her for virtues she does not yet have:

> *Say that she rail, why then I'll tell her plain*
> *She sings as sweetly as a nightingale;*
> *Say that she frown, I'll say she looks as clear*
> *As morning roses newly wash'd with dew;*
> *Say she be mute, and will not speak a word,*
> *Then I'll commend her volubility,*
> *And say she uttereth piercing eloquence;*
> *If she do bid me pack, I'll give her thanks,*
> *As though she bid me stay by her a week;*
> *If she deny to wed, I'll crave the day*
> *When I shall ask the banes, and when be*
> *married. (2.1.170–80)*

Maybe Petruchio does not quite expect the razor-sharp repartee which Kate delivers in the rest of the scene, but throughout this rollicking battle, he insists on what Brian Moss calls an "ideal picture," a performed image, of Kate's future virtue.[7] Petruchio praises his lady for her "pleasant, gamesome," and "passing courteous" disposition, "sweet as spring-time flowers" (2.1.245–46). He compliments her "mildness" and "gentle confidence" (2.1.250–51). When Baptista, Gremio, and Tranio enter, he keeps up this pretense: "She's not forward," he tells them, "but modest as the dove; / She is not hot, but temperate as the morn" (2.1.293–94). On the surface, this teasing might seem like meaningless mockery, but Petruchio explains in soliloquy that his intent is ultimately loving: He wishes to "woo [Kate] with some spirit" (2.1.169).

These images of virtue foreshadow the end of Kate's story, but they are not what ultimately moves Kate toward that final destination. In another strategy, Petruchio performs for Kate her own shrewishness back to her. In his servant Peter's words, "He kills her in her own humor" (4.1.180). This tactic appears at the wedding scene, what Alvin Kernan calls "Petruchio's greatest play."[8] The groom arrives late to the event and in an outrageous costume: "A new hat and an old jerkin; a pair of old breeches thrice turn'd; a pair of boots that have been candle-cases, one buckled, another lac'd; an old rusty ta'en out of the town armory, with a broken hilt, and chapeless" (3.2.43–48). Baptista balks at his appearance, but Petruchio waves away the father's complaint:

To me she's married, not unto my clothes.
Could I repair what she will wear in me,
As I can change these poor accoutrements,
'Twere well for Kate, and better
    for myself. (3.2.115, 117–20)

Now the meaning of Petruchio's antics is plain: It is easy to change one's external presentation (a truth the audience learns in full from Bianca's affectations). But the inner condition is not so effortlessly changed, and this is the condition

3 UNOFFENSIVE THEMES IN *THE TAMING OF THE SHREW*

that matters to marriage. Establishing this analogy between outer dress and inner virtue, the audience infers that Petruchio's mad appearance is an image of Kate's disheveled and unruly interior life. Thus Tranio rightly observes that Petruchio "hath some meaning in his mad attire" (3.2.124).

As we'd expect, imagination proves crucial at Kate's ultimate transformation scene in act four, scene 5, the famous "sun and moon" dialogue, when Shakespeare brings Petruchio's mad behavior to its culmination. On the road back to Padua, Petruchio tries his last and most extravagant experiment yet:

PETRUCHIO. *Come on a' God's name, once more toward our father's.*
Good Lord, how bright and goodly shines the moon!

KATHERINA. *The moon! the sun—it is not moonlight now.*

PETRUCHIO. *I say it is the moon that shines so bright.*

KATHERINA. *I know it is the sun that shines so bright.*

PETRUCHIO. *Now by my mother's son, and that's myself,*
    It shall be moon, or star, or what I list,
    Or ere I journey to your father's house.—
    Go on, and fetch our horses back again.—
Evermore cross'd and cross'd, nothing but cross'd!

HORTENSIO. *Say as he says, or we shall never go.*

KATHERINA. *Forward, I pray, since we have come so far,*
  And be it moon, or sun, or what you please;
  And if you please to call it a rush-candle,
  Henceforth I vow it shall be so for me. (4.5.1–15)

It is tempting to read this scene as Kate's final collapse after so much starvation, sleeplessness, and brainwashing—a kind of defeat in submission. Trevor McNeely calls the scene a hallucination which epitomizes the whole play, a phantasmal breakdown in which we with Kate "succumb under the assault" and "accept the impossible."[9] But isn't this hallucination thesis implausible given the fireworks display of language and imaginative banter that Kate issues throughout the rest of the scene? When Vincentio, the father of Lucentio, arrives, Petruchio and Kate join together in pure imaginative play. "Good morrow, gentle mistress," Petruchio greets Vincentio, much to the man's perplexity. "Where away? / Tell me. Sweet Kate, and tell me truly too, / Hast thou beheld a fresher gentlewoman?" (4.5.27–29). Kate joins in the game:

Young budding virgin, fair, and fresh, and sweet,
Whither away, or [where] is thy abode?
Happy the parents of so fair a child!
Happier the man whom favorable stars
Allots thee for his lovely bedfellow! (4.5.37–41)

3 UNOFFENSIVE THEMES IN *THE TAMING OF THE SHREW*

It seems unlikely that a person on the cusp of a mental breakdown would be able to spin such fanciful and mellifluous verbiage off the cuff. Petruchio then changes the game, and Kate plays along:

> PETRUCHIO. *Why, how now, Kate, I hope thou art not mad.*
> *This is a man, old, wrinkled, faded, withered,*
> *And not a maiden, as thou say'st he is.*
>
> KATHERINA. *Pardon, old father, my mistaking eyes,*
> *That have been so bedazzled with the sun,*
> *That every thing I look on seemeth green.* (4.5.42–47)

Indeed, the audience, too, is "bedazzled" by the transformation that takes place. In one moment, Kate is battling the seemingly senseless obstinacy of her husband. In the next, she is engaging with him in a spirited repartee of wit and imagination. Kate has become, as Vincentio observes, a "merry mistress" (4.5.53).

What is the cause of Kate's transformation? What does she see that we do not yet see? This scene is what we might call Kate's "imaginative turn." Some momentous event of understanding happens in the silence between lines eleven (Horatio's admonition: "Say as he says, or we shall never go") and twelve (Kate's "Forward, I pray"). The deeper meaning of Petruchio's belligerence finally clicks: She too has been violent toward others (e.g., 2.1.22, 219, 142–59). She too has refused progress (3.2.207–14). Kate can now see these things. She concedes then, not to a husband tyrant, but because she now recognizes the antagonism as a theatrical role. She submits to the rules of the game as a game. Hence the spirit of play.

Play is, of course, what Kate has been unable to do up until this point. Looking back on the development of her character, we see that Kate's shrewishness was always tinged by a deeper problem of insecurity. We remember her frustration with her father ("I pray you, [father], is it your will / To make a stale of me amongst these mates?"), her embarrassment at the wedding ("Now must the world point at poor Katherina"), and her general fear of public disrespect ("I see a woman may be made a fool, / If she had not a spirit to resist") (1.1.57–58; 2.2.18; 3.2.220–21). What is the cause of this insecurity and Kate's spirit of resistance? Is it not, as Peter Saccio perceptively notes, "Bianca's popularity and Baptista's favouritism"?[10] The audience catches a hint of these dynamics at the beginning of 2.1:

KATHERINA. *Of all thy suitors here I charge*
  [thee] tell
Whom thou lov'st best; see thou dissemble not.

BIANCA. *Believe me, sister, of all the men alive*
I never yet beheld that special face
Which I could fancy more than any other.

3 UNOFFENSIVE THEMES IN *THE TAMING OF THE SHREW*

KATHERINA. Minion, thou liest. Is't not Hortensio?
BIANCA. If you affect him, sister, here I swear
I'll plead for you myself, but you shall have him.

KATHERINA. O then belike you fancy riches more:
You will have Gremio to keep you fair.

BIANCA. Is it for him you do envy me so?
Nay then you jest, and now I well perceive
You have but jested with me all this while.
I prithee, sister Kate, untie my hands.

KATHERINA. If that be jest, then all the rest was so.

Strikes her. (2.1.8–22)

Kate wants to know which man Bianca likes and cannot accept her pretense of detached disinterest in the scrambling and scrabbling of her suitors. Bianca uses this opportunity as a way to tease Katherina and reassert her privilege as the beloved daughter and coveted lady: When Kate asks Bianca whether she fancies Gremio, Bianca balks ("Is it for him you do envy me so? / Nay then you jest"). But Kate sees through this clever deflection: Pretending that she is the brunt of the joke, Bianca has jestingly exposed Kate's insecurity. No wonder Kate strikes Bianca at this moment, and no wonder she strikes out at others. Her scorn is a preventative measure against those who would mistreat her: "A woman may be made a fool, / If she had not a spirit to resist."

But at the end of the story, the audience watches that old insecurity leave Kate. In act 5, scene 1, we encounter a similar scene of impasse, but mark the difference in Kate's response to it. After the inevitable debacle between Lucentio and his father, Vincentio, is sorted out and Gremio resigns his quest for Bianca, Petruchio and Kate are left alone in the street outside Lucentio's house. Petruchio asks for a kiss (at the time, a highly indecorous thing in public). Kate demurs, then accepts:

> KATHERINA. *Husband, let's follow, to see the end of this ado.*
>
> PETRUCHIO. *First kiss me, Kate, and we will.*
>
> KATHERINA. *What, in the midst of the street?*
>
> PETRUCHIO. *What, are thou asham'd of me?*
>
> KATHERINA. *No, sir, but asham'd to kiss.*
>
> PETRUCHIO. *Why then let's home again. Come, sirrah, let's away.*
>
> KATHERINA. *Nay, I will give thee a kiss; now pray thee, love, stay.* (5.1.142–48)

3 UNOFFENSIVE THEMES IN *THE TAMING OF THE SHREW*

Kate's response is a sign that she is no longer haunted by the specter of public opinion. One may be tempted to read Petruchio's lines as a return to the old autocracy, but Kate's affectionate address ("now pray thee, love, stay") suggests that her husband's bluster is more playful coercion than high-handed command. Petruchio's performance is over, and Kate grants his wish—not out of fear or compulsion, but out of caring.

This reading of act 4, scene 5 lends itself to an unironic interpretation of Kate's infamous last speech in 5.2. Having proven her fidelity in Petruchio's contest, Kate delivers a long address on the importance of self-giving, ending with an unequivocal gesture of love.

> ... *place your hands below your husband's foot;*
> *In token of which duty, if he please,*
> *My hand is ready, may it do him ease. (5.2.177–79)*

Shakespearean scholars have noted how Kate's gesture of putting her hand under Petruchio's boot is not a random act of self-degradation, but a traditional part of the Sarum Rite at the solemnization of marriage.[11] So while Kate and Petruchio are formally married in act 3, scene 2, they are emotionally and spiritually married in act 5, scene.2. Kate's love for her husband has come to fruition. Here the comedic *dénouement* results in more than slavish obedience to convention: Kate finds a "new-built virtue" (5.2.118).

Some Nonconclusive Notes

1. The passions pose a human problem.
2. Reason alone is a bad chaperone for the passions.
3. Imagination informs right action.

Admittedly, these points leave certain problem passages unaddressed. They pass over genuinely unsettling elements. Auden was right about the disconcerting side of *The Shrew*: Many scenes are head scratchers; several speeches make us deeply uncomfortable, and rightly so. Who, for example, can countenance Petruchio's foul behavior during his first meeting with Kate (in act 2, scene 1)? Who would approve of the way he starves her during their wacko honeymoon (4.1.170–78)? But we must deal with these problems elsewhere. The point is not to deny the many uncomfortable incidents which pepper the play with controversy. The aim rather is to acknowledge those genuinely interesting themes which transcend farce: the nature of the soul and the means of moral transformation.

At the end of the day, is *The Shrew* merely a foolish farce about men ruling women? I don't think so. Shakespeare's thematic patterns suggest a bigger philosophy of how people change. The play illustrates what goes wrong when we let our base feelings run our lives, for like Kate and Lucentio and Sly, we become irrational, irascible, and unruly when our viscera take control. We live out of sorts with ourselves and out of relationship with others.

Sometimes we try to conquer these passions through ideas alone, and though that seems better than nothing, we often find that sheer mental effort proves fruitless. Why? Because as Shakespeare so helpfully illustrates, ideas garner strength from the imagination. Thinking must draw its energies from the will. Like Katherina, we need to be awakened to truth in our souls and not just in our minds. And just as Kate learns love through the theatrical antics of Petruchio, so too our souls can be tamed through imagination.

CHAPTER THREE

A THOUSAND SEVERAL TONGUES

There is another man within me that's angry with me.

Sir Thomas Browne, *Religio Medici*, 2.7

It seems natural for the human mind to figure the conscience in metaphors of antagonism. We talk of guilt's "attacks" and "pangs" and speak of conscience as a "scourge." Juvenal famously pictures guilt as a torturer bearing an "unseen whip."[1] And St. Augustine refers to a "grand struggle" in his "inner house."[2] A person with a conscience is never just one person. A conscience is a colloquy.

Shakespeare's *Richard III* is one of the greatest works of literature about guilt because it reveals both what a burdened conscience feels like and the price one must pay to ignore it. The plot follows the bloody machinations of Richard, the Duke of Gloucester, who wins the throne of England by murderous means after the death of his brother King Edward IV. Richard is responsible for the deaths of noblemen, relatives, even his own wife Queen Anne, and it is not until the Earl of

Richmond challenges Richard's kingship that hope begins to dawn for England. As these sins weigh on Richard, his conscience wakes up, and a colloquy of voices holds court.

The most powerful dramatization of the divided mind arrives in act 5, scene 3, on the eve of battle at Bosworth Field. In the still of the night, Richard is haunted by the souls slain in his terrible intrigues, who all condemn him for his treachery. After the visitation, the crooked king is left alone with himself (or perhaps we should say, left alone with himselves):

> *What do I fear? Myself? There's none else by.*
> *Richard loves Richard, that is, I am I.*
> *Is there a murtherer here? No. Yes, I am.*
> *Then fly. What, from myself? Great reason why—*
> *Lest I revenge. What, myself upon myself?*
> *Alack, I love myself. Wherefore? For any good*
> *That I myself have done unto myself?*
> *O, no! Alas, I rather hate myself*
> *For hateful deeds committed by myself.*
> *I am a villain; yet I lie, I am not.*
> *Fool, of thyself speak well; fool, do not flatter:*
> *My conscience hath a thousand several tongues,*
> *And every tongue brings in a several tale,*
> *And every tale condemns me for a villain. (5.3.182–95)*

As Richard takes an inward turn, he begins to argue with himself, a debate which glimmers in a dozen reflexive references (i.e., "me," "myself," "thyself," and "Richard"). In this short passage, the king comforts himself three times, contradicts himself four times, berates himself five times, and questions himself a total of seven times. As Agnes Heller puts it, "[H]is personality is split: one half loves the other half, one half hates the other half, one half judges or confirms the other half."[3] The terse style of this speech and its choppy staccato sentences reveal the intense debate going on in Richard's soul.

At this crux, Richard tries to shake off the force of this condemnation, being from the beginning "determined to prove a villain" (1.1.30). But how does he attempt this? How does he try to silence the "thousand several tongues" of conscience? By boldly declaring another arbitrator: his own sheer power. Prior to his final war speech, Richard dismisses the claims of moral intuition altogether. "Conscience is but a word that cowards use," he sneers, "Devis'd at first to keep the strong in awe: / Our strong arms be our conscience, swords our law" (5.3.309–11). Henceforward, might will make right for Richard. Power will lead and judge.

Of course, this plan never works out for him because the last vestiges of Richard's humanity can never finally shake off the impulse to appeal to some external good. Note, for example, the confused final battle cry Richard issues in act 5, scene 3:

> A thousand hearts are great within my bosom.
> Advance our standards, set upon our foes.
> Our ancient word of courage, fair Saint George,

> *Inspire us with the spleen of fiery dragons!*
> *Upon them! Victory sits on our helms. (5.3.347–51)*

If you know your English legendarium, you will pick up on Richard's slip. Notice how in lines 349 and 350 the king calls simultaneously for "courage" (a virtue) and "spleen" (a vice)—invoking both "Saint George" (England's patron saint) and the "fiery dragon" (the terrible beast that Saint George slew). Talk about a muddled mind. Richard cannot escape the claims of conscience, so in the heat of the moment, he appeals both to good and evil, heroism and malice.

The king certainly issues a lot of bravado in these lines, but is he really confident after all? And who are these "thousand hearts" within Richard? Perhaps conscience's "thousand several tongues" bound and gagged. Shakespeare's audience hardly believes the bluster, for by this point in the play we know that these tribunal voices all "condemn [Richard] for a villain." The Earl of Oxford repeats the number trope again in act 5, scene 2: "Every man's conscience," he says, "is a thousand men, / To fight against this [Richard's] guilty homicide" (17–18). Richard tries to silence the colloquy, but this decision only ensures his ruin.

Clearly, conscience in *Richard III* represents an objective authority that transcends the individual mind. Richard's guilt channels the voice of some authoritative Other—not merely his own private, moral deliberation. Such is the ancient view of the conscience which grounds all moral thinking in the first principles of practical reason, but ever since the

Enlightenment, philosophers have looked on this transcendental quality of moral feeling with increasing suspicion. In his *Leviathan*, Thomas Hobbes, for instance, argues that conscience is nothing more than personal judgment.[4] The great economist Adam Smith likewise contends that conscience is simply human inference in moral reasoning, what he calls "the supposed impartial spectator": Our moments of conscience are essentially speculations about the moral judgments of others.[5] Further down the slope of subjectivity, the philosopher Hegel goes so far as to argue that conscience mainly reflects a particular culture's values and that these values must occasionally be abrogated for the sake of historical progress: The "World-historical individual" must transcend contemporary mores and bring about a new social order.[6] In short, for many modern thinkers after Shakespeare, conscience is primarily a private affair. They reduce the "moral compass" to individual feeling or social speculation.

But we see where this dismal trajectory leaves us: a mess of modern-day Richards—a society of souls who, like the tyrant king, deny the authority of the conscience yet can't escape its haunting claims. As legal thinker Robert Vischer perceptively observes, "Most students of the human condition" today have discarded the idea that the conscience is a "deposit of absolute and universal moral truth." Yet this same number, he says, will "intuitively resist" the conclusion that conscience is "personal preference."[7] So which is it? Is conscience a private affair? Is it maybe a weird by-product of evolution? Or does its power stem from somewhere else?

As Shakespeare teaches us in *Richard III*, one answer to that question leads to life, and the other leads to death. Richard's "thousand several tongues" are not just the fanciful projection of his wild imagination. They constitute the real moral voice of the multitude. To ignore those voices is to be divided and destroyed.

CHAPTER FOUR

THE CONVERSE OF BREATH

Inanis verborum torrens.

Quintilian, *Institutes of Oratory*

Love's *Labour's Lost* may be Shakespeare's wackiest comedy. Edit that: *Labour's* takes the cake as wackiest comedy, and a quick synopsis proves the point.

The story goes like this: At the start of the play, the King of Navarre and three noblemen all swear off romantic interests to pursue the glories of academic prestige and save their names from the ravages of time. But soon four ladies arrive from France with a written treaty concerning the disputed region of Aquitaine. Both Navarre and France claim the territory by right, so after a brief conference with the four lords, the princess of France agrees to produce proof of France's war-payments. By this point, however, firm diplomacy is out the window for the king of Navarre since he and his men have all instantly fallen in love with the four ladies (thankfully without overlap). None of the nobles want the others discovering his secret passion, but in a brilliant scene of triple-layered eavesdropping, they all discover each other's love poetry and confess to breaking their oaths. Just as firmly as they swear off womankind, they now swear to win these ladies' hearts. The four set off on a wacky love-quest, which includes (among other strange events) Russian disguises, confused identities, and corny skits with Holofernes—a pedant who has to be one of the silliest teachers in literature. For a while, the ladies seem to be along for the ride, but at the very end of the play, this hurly-burly is interrupted by a messenger bearing sad news from France: word of the king's death. With this cold wave of sobriety, the company confesses their excessive silliness and devil-may-care antics. The ladies depart for home, but there is some hope that these new romances will rekindle after the men spend a full year in ascetic retreat, forging honest character.

Obviously, *Labour's* is an outlier as far as comedies go. Its plot structure breaks the typical sequence of initial exposition, blocking complication, and romantic resolution. Death bookends the play. We begin in the shadow of "cormorant devouring time" and four noblemen's questionable plan to escape "the disgrace of death" through learning (1.1.3), and we end in the "mourning house" (5.2.808). In what Emma Smith describes as a "reverse deus ex machina," the last scene introduces a brand-new character, Monsieur Marcade, who comes not to bring the couples together with good news, but to separate them with bad news.[1] Instead of an unlikely happy ending, we get an unlikely unhappy one.

THE CONVERSE OF BREATH

Despite its strange dramatic shape, *Love's Labour's Lost* is clearly a play about the importance of honest speech. At each major turning point, there is some slippage between words and reality: broken oaths, disputed treaties, misdelivered mail, syrupy sonnets, mawkish doting, and failed theater. In a story-world of words that do not often hit their targets, we learn the importance of words that do.

The princess seems to understand the imperative of honest speech better than any other character in the play. Why be honest? Because dishonesty wastes words:

> BOYET. *Be now as prodigal of all dear grace*
> *As Nature was in making graces dear,*
> *When she did starve the general world beside*
> *And prodigally gave them all to you.*
>
> PRINCESS. *Good Lord Boyet, my beauty, though but mean,*
> *Needs not the painted flourish of your praise:*
> *Beauty is bought by judgement of the eye,*
> *Not utt'red by base sale of chapmen's tongues.*
> *I am less proud to hear you tell my worth*
> *Than you much willing to be counted wise*
> *In spending your wit in the praise of mine.* (2.1.9–19)

Notice the language of commerce the princess adopts to make her point about exaggerative rhetoric. In praising his lady with hyperbole, Boyet is like a "chapman" or merchant who uses inflated speech to peddle his wares. True beauty sells itself and is "bought by judgement," the princess claims, so Boyet's overstatement proves a needless expenditure of mental energy. The princess invites Boyet to move from dishonest pretty speech to honest plain speech, and here we witness a shift from the poetic to the prosaic even on the level of form. This loquacious lackey's lines have all the bounce of lively iambic pentameter, but in the princess's reply, her feet stray into a much more conversational rhythm, first with heavy stresses ("Needs not"), then with a bouncing meter ("Beau-ty is bought") and last with a scattering of accents (e.g., "I am less proud" and "much willing to be count-ed wise"). Boyet uses "painted flourish," the princess observes, but she would rather pass on such "base sale." Honest prose is better than insincere poetry.

By the end of the play, her lover, Lord Berowne, also promises to grow a bit thriftier with his words:

> O, *never will I trust to speeches penn'd,*
> *Nor to the motion of a schoolboy's tongue,*
> *Nor never come in vizard to my friend,*
> *Nor woo in rhyme . . .*
> *. . . and I here protest,*
> *By this white glove (how white the hand, God knows!),*
> *Henceforth my wooing mind shall be express'd*
> *In russet yeas and honest kersey noes.*
> *And, to begin, wench, so God help me law!*
> *My love to thee is sound, sans crack or flaw.*
> *(5.2.402–5, 410–15)*

Berowne grasps the need for plain and honest words, and he expresses this conviction in an echo of Christ's Sermon on the Mount: "Russet yeas and honest kersey noes" ("But let your communication be, Yea, yea; Nay, nay: for whatsoever is more than these cometh from evil").[2] Ironically, Berowne alludes to this Scripture about not swearing oaths on things even as he swears on his lady's "white glove." But we have some hope for this loquacious lord. At least he wants to be reformed.

Living in a world of jargon, jingles, and twitterspeak twetiquette, some of us wish our historical moment had a serious problem with flowery Elizabethan prolixity—the "painted flourish" and the "schoolboy's tongue." It might be nice for a change to rub shoulders with some overzealous humanists: lovers too fond of sonnets, pastors too prone to learned metaphors, administrators too steeped in Latin. Still, don't we know something of the general problem of dishonest speech in both its highbrow and lowbrow forms?

Take, for instance, the current plague on academic discourse, a scene even more bewildering than the school of Holofernes. In *Fools, Firebrands, and Frauds*, Roger Scruton rightly describes the lingo of today's university intelligentsia as a "new and fortified language," a dizzying and impenetrable vocabulary that attempts to articulate its own revolutionary aims through a shift in linguistic consciousness. Academia's bizarre brand of newspeak forms a lexical barricade, a fence of words refusing debate "except in terms that are barely intelligible to those who have not renounced their capacity to think about them."³ Today's humanities students may not face the same barrage of Latinisms and inkhorn terms as Shakespeare's day, but they do encounter language used as a means of pedantic power, a cloak, a screen, a prop. Take this paragraph from Louis Althusser, which might spring upon some unsuspecting victim in critical theory class:

> *Overdetermination designates the following essential quality of contradiction: the reflection in contradiction itself of its conditions of existence, that is, of its situation in the structure in dominance of the complex whole. This is not a univocal "situation." It is not just its situation "in principle" (the one it occupies in the hierarchy of instances in relation to the determinant instance: in society, the economy) nor just its situation "in fact" (whether, in the phrase under consideration, it is dominant or subordinate) but the relation of this situation in fact to this situation in principle, that is, the very relation which makes of this situation in fact a "variation" of the—"invariant"—structure, in dominance, of the totality.*⁴

Here Holofernian bombast meets Marxist gobbledygook. Academic writing today is awash with jargon and nominalizations, words like "overdetermination" and "dominance"—a heap of fossilized verbs piling up like a boneyard of static abstractions. Whatever the author may be trying to say in this passage, the actual effect is one characterized by quasi-militaristic defensiveness. Like a moving phalanx of raised shields, this steel-gray speech deflects counterargument (and comprehension).

And then there is the "chapman's tongue" of advertising, when marketers say very little, yet manage to say it with a lot of gusto. We eat epic burgers; we buy cars at insanely low rates. Technologists offer empowering business solutions, while online universities promise to help you unleash your potential. Such catchphrases might be penned by a latter-day Boyet. They sound snappy, but the zest is "painted flourish." And the princess teaches us to recognize this "base sale" by better "judgement." Consumers must learn to discern the beautiful from the banal.

What's the cure for dishonest speech? Occasionally, we need a good jeremiad about the plight of contemporary discourse. A prophetic word from Jacques Barzun, Neil Postman, or Sven Birkerts does us good.[6] But it's interesting to note that the dramatic turn towards honesty in *Love's Labours' Lost* doesn't arrive through academic argument. The only thing which puts an end to Navarre's madcap party is the sudden news of death: the lords' honest encounter with the gravity and contingency of their immediate situation. In short, Berowne and his gang need to grow up. The party antics stop only when life ceases to be a party, only after love requires a modicum of seriousness. This swift, sober turn at the end of the play may seem like a strange move on the comedian's part, but the rhetorical principle is perfectly plain: There is a proportionality between the gravity of our words and the gravity of our world. Honest life and honest language go hand in hand.

Much of the time, our communication problems lie downstream from character problems. The apathetic adolescent speaks in the burbles and gurgles of teenage talk because he rides a daily runnel of streaming videos and music. The soapy politico deals out oily compliments because he lives in a world of palm-greasing. But we can improve our prose by seeking to improve our persons. As we pursue a virtuous life, we will consequently attend to the merits of our speech.

CHAPTER FIVE

MIDSUMMER: A CASE STUDY IN POETIC IMAGINATION

> *So far as I can make out from the OED, this more positive sense of the word ["imagination"] in English practically begins here.*
>
> Northrop Frye, *A Midsummer Night's Dream*

Light comedy is likely the first genre that comes to mind when reading Shakespeare's *A Midsummer Night's Dream*, a play which strikes some critics more as superficial fantasy than deep drama à la *Macbeth*, *Coriolanus*, and *The Winter's Tale*. The German poet A. W. Schlegel, for example, once described this comedy as "farcical adventures of folly."[1] And then there was the famous diarist, Samuel Pepys, who called *Midsummer* "the most insipid ridiculous play that [he] ever saw in [his] life."[2] Certainly, there is something right about the "light fiction" label: A light and gamesome spirit pervades Shakespeare's plot, not a dense and philosophical one. But is it really fair to consign this comedy to the category "fluff"? Not, I think, if we pay attention to the story's subtle, playful insights into the nature of poetry and the power of imagination—a wisdom which emerges quietly but forcefully through Shakespeare's art of dialogue.

Toward the end of the play, just after the magical escapades of the forest—the whole mêlée of fairy tricks and mixed-up lovers—the worldly Duke Theseus is having a chat with his bride-to-be, Hippolyta, and in the midst of this exchange, he comments skeptically on the lovers' wild and fanciful story. A funny thing happens in this sequence. In the same breath that Theseus dismisses these fantastical reports as "antique fables" and "fairy toys" of the imagination—essentially, the crazy made-up stuff of poetry—he produces what is arguably one of the most illuminating descriptions of poetic art in the history of English literature:

> *The poet's eye, in fine frenzy rolling,*
> *Doth glance from heaven to earth, from earth to heaven;*
> *And as imagination bodies forth*
> *The forms of things unknown, the poet's pen*
> *Turns them to shapes and gives to airy nothing*
> *A local habitation and a name.* (5.1.12–17)

Poet Malcolm Guite notes the ironies that pervade this passage.[3] Even as the duke dismisses the work of the poet as the "tricks" of "seething brains," he articulates with striking economy and piercing lucidity the nature and the aims of literary creativity. Even as he looks with a wary eye on the "poet's pen," he lapses into brilliant metaphor and impeccable blank verse. In a word, Theseus understands the power of poetry (even if he doesn't trust it): The poet takes what is "unknown" and makes it known through an image, "a local habitation." He traces the "forms of things unknown" and gives them "shapes" which, the duke says, "apprehend / More than cool reason ever comprehends". Of course, the duke means this statement in a disapproving way. He means, in other words, that imaginings "apprehend / More" than what actually is. But by a fascinating irony, Guite observes, Theseus "concedes almost everything his reason hopes to deny." Through the "shapes" of embodied ideas, poetry allows us to encounter truths that otherwise would hang up in the clouds as airy, abstract mysteries.

Shakespeare sustains the theme of images and transformation through the rest of the dialogue. On the surface-level of the conversation, Hippolyta contradicts the duke's skepticism, but in another register, she affirms the literary philosophy he unwittingly (yet so eloquently) articulates:

> *But all the story of the night told over,*
> *And all their minds transfigur'd so together,*
> *More witnesseth than fancy's images,*
> *And grows to something of great constancy;*
> *But howsoever, strange and admirable. (5.1.21–27)*

"Ok, Theseus," Hippolyta seems to be saying, "I know the lovers' story seems like madness, but think about it: They all report the same thing, and that fact alone lends them credibility, even though the events themselves are extraordinary." Might not the critic offer a similar defense of the poet's fictions? Though great stories sometimes seem like lunacy, over time they prove "something of great constancy." After all, The *Iliad* and *The Canterbury Tales* contain more than "fancy's images." These stories forge a common literary heritage, which "transfigures" the minds of many readers. With this "strange and admirable" vision, Guite says, "We see both what the artist sees and what they see through the things they see."[4] The poet's art images and embodies "things unknown." It also possesses the power to "transfigure" us.

Shakespeare may have derived these thoughts on the poetic imagination from any number of sources, but in Stephen Greenblatt's judgment, *Midsummer* act 5, scene 1 provides convincing evidence that Shakespeare must have read Sir Philip Sidney's *Defense of Poetry*—what is certainly the most important piece of literary criticism of the Elizabethan era.[5] Like Theseus, Sidney speaks of poetry as the art of imaging: "Poesy," he writes, "is an art of imitation . . . a representing, counterfeiting, or figuring forth—to speak metaphorically, a speaking picture—with this end, to teach and delight."[6] In other words, the form of the literary work itself exercises a rhetorical influence. Yes, literature "teaches," Sidney says, but it does not primarily teach through moral statements about the good life. Instead, he explains, the power of the poet arrives through a vivid and enticing picture of the good, which draws the soul toward virtue:

A CASE STUDY IN POETIC IMAGINATION

Whatsoever the philosopher saith should be done, he giveth a perfect picture of it in some one by whom he presupposeth it was done, so as he coupleth the general notion with the particular example. A perfect picture I say, for he yieldeth to the powers of the mind an image of that whereof the philosopher bestoweth but a wordish description, which doth neither strike, pierce, nor possess the sight of the soul so much as that other doth.

In Sidney's analysis, the difference between philosophy and poetry is the difference between telling and showing. The philosopher, he says, is often like one in the position of trying to describe an elephant or rhinoceros to a man who has never seen one, or an architect trying to put into words the look of a gorgeous palace. Such a person "might well make the hearer able to repeat, as it were by rote, all he had heard," but the teller "should never satisfy [the listener's] inward conceits with being witness to itself of a true lively knowledge." The philosopher's "learned definition" cannot "strike, pierce" or "possess the sight of the soul." It must necessarily "lie dark before the imaginative and judging power" unless "illuminated or figured forth by the speaking picture of poesy."[7] In other words, poetry accomplishes its teaching function by drawing the soul into affective contemplation of a creative imitation, an artistic word-picture of human action and its consequences. Poetic images reveal wisdom through the action of concrete particulars which contain embedded universals.

Whatever we think about Sidney's treatment of the philosopher, we notice something true in his analysis of the poet. All poetic art is inescapably "transfigurative." All poetic art "pictures." All poetic art persuades. Naturally, we disdain certain overt forms of didacticism: the kind of book that makes story merely an aesthetic husk for a moral kernel. But we recognize that literature carries an inescapable, rhetorical element, if only because literary images themselves contain persuasive power. Indeed, most of the time, the poet does not have to tell us that a thing is good or bad at all. He simply shows us the thing through drama, through plot, through vivid description, and we see the thing for what it is. This intuitional mode of teaching explains why stories and poems hold such incredible educative potential: Many people who like stories have no conscious interest in moral edification, yet they still by nature love the look of the Good. As such readers behold and receive the Good "bodied" in the "local habitation" of great books, they learn to love it. They grow in wisdom, Sidney says, "as if they took their medicine of cherries."[8]

Of course, Sidney and Shakespeare understood the dangers of literary moralism. Poets and novelists and dramatists should never use imaginative literature merely as a vehicle for moral messages. There remains, after all, a glorious uselessness about great novels and poems, and we believe that the pleasure of reading good books will always constitute its own reward. Still, do we really believe that the greatest works of verbal art have no implicit moral messages, no transfigurative power? Such a claim would run against our common experience as readers. Even after a superficial reading of *Jane Eyre*, for instance, most people like Helen Burns and dislike Mr. Brocklehurst. At the gripping *dénouement* of *To Kill a Mockingbird*, we cheer for Atticus Finch (or at least we should) because we have seen something noble and good in his character. Great novels like these persuade, but they don't persuade by way of didactic *sententiae*. The form of the work itself persuades. Poetic pictures, not polemics, convince the reader.

Of course, we can ignore this transfigurative element of literature all day long, pretending all the while that, as Archibald MacLeish would have it, "a poem should not mean / But be."[9] But the pictures will not stop speaking. They cannot help but do so. The question is what those images are saying.

I find it interesting that Renaissance poets like Shakespeare, Sidney, Edmund Spenser, Ben Jonson, Thomas Dekker, John Marston, and Robert Greene had no problem reconciling the artistic and ethical aims of imaginative writing. In fact, C. S. Lewis goes so far as to say that the sixteenth-century classics were written by men and women "to whom the distinction between poetry and rhetoric, in its modern form, would have been meaningless."[10] Brian Vickers, a scholar and teacher from University College London, puts the same point a little more starkly: "There were no purely aesthetic theories" in the Elizabethan world, "no poetics addressed to the artwork as a formal entity detached from its intended effect on the reader."[11] Imagination and moral transformation went hand in hand.

As moderns we usually think that our age is better equipped to handle subtlety and complexity than our benighted predecessors, but when it comes to the topic of literary "transfiguration," I wonder if the reverse isn't actually the case. The Elizabethan mind developed a highly sophisticated theory of poetic knowledge, and for this reason alone, it may be worth returning to that time period, not only to understand Shakespeare better, but also to acquire another vantage on our own literary projects.

CHAPTER SIX

HENRY V AND THE SHRUGGING SHAKESPEARE

> "Which is your favourite play? I wonder
> if it's the same as mine?"
> "Henry the Fifth," said Mr Grice.
> "Joy!" cried Clarissa, "It is!"
>
> Virginia Woolf, *The Voyage Out*

In *Henry V*, Shakespeare could be accused of playing a moral shell game. "Is Harry a Christian king?" Certainly, one could easily cherry-pick enough scenes and speeches to argue a convincing yea. The play is full of them. We have Henry's claim to Christian leadership (1.1.241), his public piety (4.8.107–108), and his private, earnest prayer (4.1.293–94). We even get this high praise after Agincourt from the seemingly trustworthy Chorus:

> Where that his lords desire him to have borne
> His bruised helmet and his bended sword
> Before him through the city. He forbids it,
> Being free from vainness and self-glorious pride;

> *Giving full trophy, signal, and ostent*
> *Quite from himself to God. (5.Prologue.17–22)*

But there are other, less flattering moments for Henry. When provoked, the king often shows an autocratic side. One thinks of the chilling violence in that retort to the Dauphin's tennis-ball joke in act 1, scene 1: "Many a thousand widows," the king swears, "shall this his mock mock out of their dear husbands." France's jest will "mock mothers from their sons, mock castles down" (284–86). And what about Harry's infernal rhetoric at the gates of Harfleur, where he warns of "waste and desolation" should the people fail to surrender (3.3.18)?

> *Why, in a moment look to see*
> *The blind and bloody soldier with foul hand*
> *[Defile] the locks of your shrill-shriking daughters;*
> *Your fathers taken by the silver beards,*
> *And their most reverend heads dash'd to the walls;*
> *Your naked infants spitted upon pikes,*
> *Whiles the mad mothers with their howls confus'd*
> *Do break the clouds, as did the wives of Jewry*
> *At Herod's bloody-hunting slaughter-men. (3.3.33–41)*

Would a truly "Christian king" threaten the virgin daughters or liken himself to the Christ-child's murderous assailant? Would a pious monarch allow another Massacre of the Innocents? And Henry's violence isn't limited to speech: In a drastic breach of conduct (4.7.1–2), Henry orders his soldiers to "cut the throats" of all the captives (63), that no one "taste ... mercy" (65). Shakespeare withholds none of the controversial elements of Agincourt from Holinshed's Chronicles, his source-text for the play. So what should we do with this seeming contradiction? How does one make sense of a play like *Henry V*?

There are different approaches to this problem. In his memorable 1977 essay, "Rabbits, Ducks, and *Henry V*," Norman Rabkin identifies three traditional ways that critics have responded to the quandary that is King Henry. The first approach, Rabkin explains, is to find a balanced reading between the idealized and demonized Henries. The king is neither an ideal Christian nor a depraved Machiavel, but something in a muddled middle—in William Hazlitt's phrase, "a very amiable monster."[1] With a second camp of readers, we might conclude that Henry remains essentially an unfinished character by the end of the play: that Shakespeare simply fails to make up his mind as to whether the king is an angel or a devil. In the words of W. H. Auden, with this play, the Bard is "getting bored."[2] The third traditional option is something like an esoteric reading: Shakespeare puts dramatic evidence on one side of the issue, but can't suppress the clues of his true feelings (though which side is the true side is more than we can say). Rabkin proposes a new fourth option. Is King Henry the exemplar of Christian kingship or the nadir of ruthless tyranny? Rabkin's playfully serious answer to this dichotomy is "Yes."

In this reading, both a good Henry and a bad Henry commend themselves as legitimate options: "Shakespeare creates a work whose ultimate power," Rabkin says, "is precisely the fact that it points in two opposite directions, virtually daring us to choose one of the two opposed interpretations it requires of us."[3] King Henry is like the duck-rabbit picture of Gestalt psychology, the critic argues. Look at the play one way, and you will see one kind of creature; look at it again, and you see something very different. Shakespeare's audience cannot see both the good king and the bad king at the same time. But both kings are there in the play and with equal suggestiveness.

Many readers have been charmed by this idea of a "shrugging Shakespeare," not just in Henry V, but in all the great plays: A gordian knot lies at the heart of each drama, and the playwright stands inaccessible behind the paradoxes. Anthony Nuttall once claimed that "we have no idea what Shakespeare thought, finally, about any major question,"[4] while Harold Bloom went one step further, doubting the very existence of a Shakespearean point-of-view: "Shakespeare seems too wise to believe anything," he maintained. His characters "do not speak either for Shakespeare or for nature."[5]

Statements like this astonish us. Isn't there (to borrow a helpful phrase from Edmund Burke) a "moral imagination" in the plays?[6] Or was Shakespeare satisfied simply to shrug at the complexity of the human condition? In a way, it's no surprise that modern readers would find traces of skepticism and proto-relativism in the pages of *Henry V*. As Marjorie Garber quips, "Every age creates its own Shakespeare."[7] But as responsible enthusiasts, we must ask ourselves whether Shakespeare's love of dramatic ambiguity is best accounted for by some deep-seated, radical skepticism or whether there isn't a more common-sense explanation of things.

In the late nineteenth century, novelist Gustave Flaubert penned this very windy letter to a friend: "When I read Shakespeare," he writes,

> *I become greater, more intelligent, and more pure. When I reach the summit of one of his plays, I seem to be on a high mountain: everything disappears and yet becomes apparent. One is no longer a man, one is an eye; new horizons arise, the perspectives stretch out to infinity.*

What makes Shakespeare great in this view is that he simply presents the world as it is, in all its grandeur, without comment. His plays impose no judgments on their subject matter: "Indeed, who can tell me what Shakespeare loved, hated, or felt?" Flaubert writes. "He is a terrifying colossus: one can scarcely believe that he was a man."[8]

Flaubert rightly praises Shakespeare's extraordinary descriptive powers, but as Wayne Booth observed almost sixty years ago, in *The Rhetoric of Fiction*, much of this business about the unknowability of Shakespeare is imprecise at best and fantastically counter-empirical at worst. Certainly, Shakespeare is demure as an author: "[He] does not barge clumsily into his works." But Booth also challenges Flaubert's wild exaggerations:

> Is [Flaubert] right when he claims that we do not know what Shakespeare loved or hated? . . . The statement is most definitely mistaken if it means that the implied author of Shakespeare's plays is neutral toward all values. We do know what this Shakespeare loved and hated; it is hard to see how he could have written his plays at all if he had refused to take a strong line on at least one or two of the seven deadly sins.

The plays figure a moral universe (albeit a strange one, full of complexity and conflict). Consequently, they contain "unmistakable violations of true neutrality," Booth argues. In the plays, we discover a moral sensibility (what Booth calls "the implied Shakespeare"), which is an ethos "thoroughly engaged with life," a mind that does not reserve judgment on "the selfish, the foolish, and the cruel."[9] How is this moral sensibility communicated? Through the form of the work itself—through the poetic techniques which shape the audience's perception of characters and events:

> Even among characters of equal moral, intellectual, or aesthetic worth, all authors inevitably take sides. A given work will be "about" a character or set of characters. It cannot possibly give equal emphasis to all, regardless of what its author believes about the desirability of fairness. Hamlet is not fair to Claudius. . . . No matter how

willing we are to admit that Claudius' story is potentially as interesting as Hamlet's, this is Hamlet's story, and it cannot do justice to the king.[10]

Many of Shakespeare's plays contain ambiguity, but Booth draws a distinction between the ambiguity of the text and the ambiguity of performance. Even if absolute authorial neutrality were possible in the text of a Shakespeare play, it would not be possible to retain that neutrality in the play's production. Every performance is an interpretation, and though a play may allow multiple interpretations of specific plot elements, a performance will have to deal with these ambiguities.[11] In other words, not only is pure neutrality and objectivity undesirable; it's impossible.

What do we draw from these observations? Two realizations: one, Shakespeare is not morally neutral. When the curtain drops at the end of a good performance, most audiences feel that they have learned something meaningful about how we ought to live. Of course, we know that a play like *Henry V* is not reducible to a didactic, moral proposition. It is a story we enjoy for its rich dramatic content: the temptation of power, the burden of the crown, and the glory of battle. But it would be wrong to say that the philosophical themes of this history are uninteresting to us. Deep attention to the play results in weighty ethical-political questions: What makes a good king? What justifies war? When is it okay to break oaths? The ethical element of the story is married to its poetic presentation. The image invites our intellects not only into uncertainty and ambiguity, but also into what Glenn Arbery has called "felt reality"—"an intelligence that increases in power the more it explores the most unbearable dimensions of joy and suffering." Didacticism has its dangers, Arbery concedes. We ought to be wary of the poet who sets out to "illustrate philosophies or popularize doctrines, political or religious" through literary art. And yet, Arbery observes, the literary imagination does not exclude moral and philosophical concerns: "In fact, it works in and with the greatest ideas precisely because they most affect human action and lead to the greatest consequences; they most inform and are informed by the intelligence of feeling."[12]

Realization number two: Authorial ambiguity is not the same thing as authorial apathy. Even where the text is silent (perhaps especially where the text is silent), Shakespeare still invites us to wade through complications and come to informed judgment. *Henry V* isn't a "Choose Your Own Ethical Adventure" story in which we arbitrarily set out to find one or another system of human values in the text. Rather, *Henry V* is a puzzle, and like all puzzles worth our time, we believe that there is a way through the enigma.

Simply put, the reader must believe that Shakespeare believed things. If one goes down the other road, one will arrive at a text with no stakes, no claims, no surprises, and for that matter, no genuine questions. In Flaubert's own words, we will discover a Shakespeare who is "no longer a man."

CHAPTER SEVEN

THE WONDER OF ARDEN

*The bright original he took,
And tore the leaf from nature's book.*

Robert Lloyd, "Shakespeare"

My favorite of Shakespeare's story-worlds is the Forest of Arden—the sweet and melancholy woodlands of *As You Like It*. Arden possesses, to my mind, something that no other Shakespearean setting, not even the magical woods of Athens or Prospero's island, achieves to quite the same degree: that palpable climate C. S. Lewis used to call a story's "weather."[1] Every time that we step across the threshold of act 2, scene 1 and find ourselves once again in the company of Duke Senior and his merry men, the exiles in the forest, we feel that we are breathing bracing, familiar air.

It is a curious thing. Sometimes I wonder why this play is the one with all the magic for me, especially since *As You Like It* is a story in which nothing particularly exciting happens. It lacks *Measure for Measure*'s moral quandaries and

The Merchant' of Venice's suspense. In fact, Shakespeare dials the drama back significantly from his source-text "Rosalynde," a prose story by Thomas Lodge containing some of the same characters, but far more violence and political intrigue. By comparison, Shakespeare's narrative seems like fluff:

1. Boy has problems. Girl has problems.
2. Boy meets girl. Both fall in love at first sight.
3. Boy runs away to the woods to escape problems; girl does too.
4. Girl (disguised) recognizes boy (not disguised), but (of course) boy does not recognize girl.
5. Attempting to teach boy the art of wooing, girl pretends to be someone pretending to be herself; antics ensue.
6. Boy and girl join exiled nobles who lounge about making music and philosophizing.
7. Miraculous events happen, even a literal *deus ex machina*.
8. All political and interpersonal problems are supernaturally rectified, and everybody falls in love. The end.

Not your obvious candidate for the Plotters Hall of Fame. Shakespeare's scheme here is "emotionally . . . untaxing," Stanley Wells says. "Its story, such as it is, is slight and can be followed without difficulty. It is written in a limpid and uncomplicated style with a high proportion of prose."[2] So I ask myself, "What makes this setting so special?" What is so enchanting about an imaginary world that boasts little of *Measure*'s ethical pyrotechnics, little of *Merchant*'s political intrigue?

Though Shakespeare clearly takes inspiration from the English Forest of Arden (the once wooded region near his boyhood home in Warwickshire), the fictional Forest of Arden is not an ordinary place like other settings in the plays—e.g., Vienna, Venice, London, Athens, Ephesus, Navarre, or Rome. Arden exists in an altogether different dimension—a world "more symbolic than geographical," to borrow Hannibal Hamlin's expression—which solicits a different side of our imaginative powers.[3] When we sit down to read Anthony Trollope or William Faulkner, we experience the tourist's thrill of riding into town on the dusty roads of Barsetshire and Yoknapatawpha. But as we cross the threshold of Arden, we experience a very different kind of literary pleasure: the joy of visiting the world of the imagination as such. Stepping into Shakespeare's "golden world" of exile, we move from poetry into the poetic mind itself. Arden is a metaphor for the imagination.

For one thing, Arden is a place of wonder. That is to say, Arden is a place where one gains a fresh intellectual contact with the world. Consider the first moment in the play that we enter the forest. In act 2, scene 1, we meet Duke Senior, a mistreated magistrate who has been exiled to the woods of Arden by his usurping brother Frederick. Like so many of Shakespeare's noble leaders, Senior has taken a bad turn on fortune's wheel, and, given the circumstances, one might expect to meet a chilly and embittered soul. But instead we greet a man marked above all by his peaceful thoughts and spiritual sensitivity. Rather than grumbling, Senior reflects on the goodness of his new, austere life in the forest and cheers his lordly retinue with the thought that maybe things aren't so bad after all:

> Now, my co-mates and brothers in exile,
> Hath not old custom made this life more sweet
> Than that of painted pomp? Are not these woods
> More free from peril than the envious court?
> Here feel we not the penalty of Adam,
> The seasons' difference, as the icy fang
> And churlish chiding of the winter's wind,
> Which when it bites and blows upon my body
> Even till I shrink with cold, I smile and say,
> "This is no flattery: these are counsellors
> That feelingly persuade me what I am."
> Sweet are the uses of adversity,
> Which like the toad, ugly and venomous,
> Wears yet a precious jewel in his head;
> And this our life, exempt from public haunt,
> Finds tongues in trees, books in the running brooks,
> Sermons in stones, and good in every thing. (2.1.1–17)

If you have ever wanted to leave the commercial sprawl of Dallas for the sanctuary of the Texas Hill Country or escape I-93 traffic and collect yourself in some quiet, coastline eatery, then you know a little of what Duke Senior is talking about. He offers a straightforward gloss on the traditional pastoral message: A simple, rural life is better than a city life because at least in the country, far from the madding crowd, you know who you are. Senior's new life in Arden might not be as comfortable as his dukedom, and it certainly isn't as glamorous. But at least from this vantage point he can now discern the extravagances and vanities of *haut monde* style for what they are—the business of "pomp," "envious" living, and "flattery." Even in political exile, the simple, humble life starts to look more attractive than his former one. Away from the miasma of worldly aims and honors, Duke Senior once again beholds the bare spiritual facts of his condition and apprehends the true cares and contingencies of precious existence. Life is frail in Arden. But then again, life is frail everywhere. Life is good in Arden. But then again, even the barest levels of being are good.

How exactly does this moral transformation take place? In Senior's analysis, the worldly soul must not only come to rationally comprehend the truth of his mortal situation. He must also come to soulfully apprehend (for lack of a better expression) the truthiness of that truth. Hence the language of sense that pervades the passage: In Arden, Senior can "feel . . . the penalty of Adam," and the elements "feelingly persuade" him of his own dependencies. This transformative process certainly involves thinking, but it is important to say that we are talking about a special kind of thinking—not a calculating, cogitating sort of thought, but that simple act of attentive beholding philosopher Josef Pieper fondly called "contemplation."[4] Duke Senior must behold what is. He probably understood some of these truths prior to his exile in Arden on an intellectual level. He probably knew that existence was precious and tentative and fleeting. Still, it took the "churlish chiding of the winter's wind" to sense those truths anew. He had to "feel" the truth again to live it.

One of our dire perennial obstacles to living well is our failure to apprehend the truth, for it is one thing to know something as an idea and a very different thing to know it through experience. This is what we mean by the ocular metaphor "seeing things as they are": Seeing rightly means both beholding the implicit order of reality and recognizing our place within it. No doubt, this task is hard, and we often forget what truth looks like, lured by the dazzle and distraction of politics, fashionable ideas, zeitgeisty slogans, and frivolous entertainment. But once we step out of the funhouse and attend again to the basic realities of our existence, we discover a world that speaks "good in every thing"—a world of rocks, canyons, oceans, clouds, and firelight, all of which "feelingly persuade" us what we are.

Furthermore, Arden is home to art and imitation. Like Duke Senior, the young hero Orlando learns to "see rightly" while in Arden, but interestingly enough, he doesn't change in the same way Duke Senior does—simply by living attentively in his new environs. Instead, he experiences transformation through an event best described as "poetic knowledge." Like Senior, Orlando discovers a life of virtue free from courtly pretense. But unlike Senior, this education arrives through artifice, not nature. If we look closely at this plotline, we can begin to recognize how fiction and imagination play an important role in the project of learning to see reality as it is.

This play opens with one man's problem of imagination: his failure to apprehend the basic social reality in which he lives and moves. Orlando, for all his virtues, does not see things correctly, and the main question of the play becomes whether this faculty of moral sight can be rehabilitated. On the one hand, Orlando displays real nobility, dignity, intelligence, charm, and unflappable courage. But as the story unfolds, Shakespeare's audience also detects the workings of vainglory—an inordinate love of a certain courtly image which has little to do with authentic virtue. From the outset, these two sides of Orlando war with one another, and, as is so often the case in moral formation, Orlando finds that his virtue is tied to a vice. Nobility battles vainglory, and we wait to see which side wins out.

The story goes like this: Orlando and Duke Senior's daughter Rosalind fall in love, though each remains unaware of the other's feelings. But soon the unstable political situation erupts, sending both lovers on separate flights to the woods—Orlando with his servant Adam, Rosalind with her cousin Celia and the court jester Touchstone. In this new, exotic world, Orlando taps into his troubadour side as he walks around the forest crafting love poetry to Rosalind and pinning it on trees. Naturally, Rosalind soon gets word of this behavior, and things look hopeful for the lovers' union. At this point, a "happily ever after" seems right around the corner.

Strangely, though, Rosalind doesn't reveal her identity to her beloved. She remains cloaked. This decision may perplex us at first. After all, Rosalind is safe in her father's company, and she has manifest proof of Orlando's undying love for her. Why then does she remain disguised? For this astonishing reason, it seems: Rosalind spies the subtle narcissism lurking beneath the charming surface of Orlando's courtly passion, and she tries to train it out of him through an ingenious experiment.

Now what exactly is Rosalind's evidence? What tips her off to Orlando's egotism? His immaculate appearance. Orlando claims that he is a languishing lover, but we laugh in act 3, scene 2 as Rosalind catalogues all the true marks of a lovesick man (none of which show up on Orlando):

> ROSALIND. *A lean cheek, which you have not; a blue eye and sunken, which you have not; a beard neglected, which you have not (but I pardon you for that, for simply your having a beard is a younger brother's revenue); then your hose should be ungarter'd, your bonnet unbanded, your sleeve unbutton'd, your shoe untied, and everything about you demonstrating a careless desolation. But you are no such man; you are rather point-device in your accoutrements, as loving yourself, than seeming the lover of any other.*
>
> ORLANDO. *Fair youth, I would I could make thee believe I love.*

THE WONDER OF ARDEN

ROSALIND. Me believe it? You may as soon make her that you love believe it, which I warrant she is apter to do than to confess she does. (3.2.373–89)

If Orlando were truly pining away, he would not look so hale and hearty. He would not dress himself in apple-pie order. But he does, and Rosalind points out the inconsistency. Is it possible that Orlando is in love with the idea of being in love? Our hero's passion, though genuine in part, possesses an air of performed gentility. Orlando truly finds himself attracted to Rosalind, but at the same time, he finds himself playing a role, the character of the gentleman lover he imagines himself to be.

Orlando's problem is ultimately a failure to rightly apprehend the life of true honor. So it follows that his cure must come through a reapprehension of that virtue. In an ironic turn of events, Rosalind offers to cure Orlando of love by pretending to be his beloved. He must learn to woo a lady by learning to woo this proxy, and in the course of this imaginative experiment, all kinds of interesting character flaws appear. Rosalind's theatrical picture of true love proves much more demanding than Orlando's chivalric daydream. At every turn, Orlando is forced to say, "Is this what love actually demands? Will my Rosalind really behave this way? Do I really want this kind of life?"

As Marjorie Garber brilliantly argues, this education, not the courtly education Orlando demanded at the beginning of the play, turns out to be the training Orlando needed all along: the chance to discover what love really is, without all the worldly egotism. We find in the end that Rosalind does not want to "cure" Orlando of true love, only love's vitiated substitute. At the beginning of the play, the hero is a dreamy-eyed romantic who "has immersed himself in a pseudo-Petrarchan fantasy world" and must learn afresh, to borrow Rosalind's words, "what 'tis to love" (5.2.83).[5] He must grow up, Garber puts it, "from a tongue-tied boy to an articulate and (relatively) self-knowledgeable husband."[6] Rosalind's experiment prepares her lover for the reality of love, the knowledge that he lacks at the beginning of the play.

Above I called Orlando's education an event of "poetic knowledge." But what is that, anyway? What do we mean by that impressive sounding term? Consider this illuminating address on the topic from the great educationalist John Senior (a genius who incidentally bears no relation to the other genius Senior in this essay!):

> *What is poetic knowledge? It is not simply expression— we are talking about an experience, and you have to experience the experience. The philosophers call this connatural knowledge—it is not abstract knowledge. Here, somebody knows something, but the only way to know what he knows is to know it yourself in the same way that he knows it. For example, you touch a hot stove, and you say, ouch. Then you ask somebody: you think stoves are hot? How do you know that? And, you say, touch it for yourself. You can repeat this kind of experi-*

> ence, but it is very dangerous. So, we have another way, and that is by doing the experience in sympathy. We don't actually do it, but we can do it in our imaginations. This is what is meant by connatural knowledge. Children do this in play, imitating animals for example. And there is a way of understanding, say, horses, through connaturality, and that is what poetry does.[7]

"Poetic knowledge" then is knowledge through indirect experience, knowledge through a simulation of reality. Upon a moment's reflection, we realize that this "connatural" form of learning is precisely what Rosalind provides for Orlando. The wisdom gained through her theatrical experiment is not "abstract knowledge," but the wisdom of second-hand living. If Orlando is to be a responsible husband and not just a warbling troubadour, he needs to know a little of what real marriage is like. But of course, he cannot know what real marriage is like firsthand without himself being married, just as a young child cannot know the pain of a hot stove firsthand without touching it. So imagination steps in: Orlando glimpses truth through the lens of a fiction as he learns to discern authentic love from that "pseudo-Petrarchan" substitute which previously captivated him. Are these imaginings mere figments, phantasies, fancies? For Orlando, they are sources of knowledge.

As John Senior's stove example makes clear, not all poetic knowledge is poetry, for here even vivid descriptions convey second-hand experience. But we believe the converse:

All poetry is poetic knowledge. So you can see why Orlando's education makes a great analogy for literary education. Admittedly, Rosalind's experiment isn't literature *stricto sensu*. But it illustrates the generic way that all forms of poetic knowledge work. Through her play-acting, Rosalind imparts wisdom connaturally. We may add that Shakespeare does the same through his play-writing.

Arden functions as a parable for the power of literary art. Just as Rosalind teaches Orlando the nature of love through a fiction, so Shakespeare's forest world teaches us to see things as they are by offering us an indirect experience of life. Here "life" does not mean the scattered thoughts and random sense impressions of our workaday lives. It signifies instead the implicit order of reality, which in Duke Senior's phrase, contains the secret of "what we are." Literature derives its genius from nature, and this is not a weakness in literature. To the contrary, it is literature's glory. To quote the eighteenth-century poet Robert Lloyd (only a little out of context), literature "tears the leaf from nature's book," granting us this advantage over direct experience: that through the poet's eyes we will finally see a world that we cannot or do not normally apprehend.[8] We behold "good in every thing."

Yes, entering Arden is like entering the ferny haunts of the imagination, for in that "leaf-fringed legend" we come to understand the role of wonder and art in discovering truth: namely, that imagination helps us apprehend truth feelingly both in nature and the indirect experience of nature provided by creative imitations. Arden's verdant plots house both the real and the imaginary, the literal and the symbolic, the natural and the connatural, so perhaps it is this fusion of poetry and plain fact that gives Arden its particular windy-wondery aura.

Whatever the case, it's a beautiful place. I can't wait to go back there.

CHAPTER EIGHT

HOW COULD BRUTUS LOVE CAESAR?

Brutus is such a puzzle.

Harold Bloom,
Shakespeare: The Invention of the Human

One of the great challenges in *Julius Caesar* is reconciling Brutus' words and his deeds: Can he really love the man he conspires against and kills? Of course, he professes to Cassius that he does (1.2.82) and to Antony (3.1.179-83) and the plebeians (3.2.17-22) that he did. All three professions may surprise us, but the speech to the plebs contains the stated reason why he slaughters Caesar: "If that friend demand why Brutus rose against Caesar," Brutus says, "this is my answer: not that I loved Caesar less, but that I loved Rome more" (3.2.21-22). For Brutus, killing Caesar constitutes an act of "love" because it serves the common good. It ends Caesar's dangerous ambition and crushes the tyrant serpent in its shell (2.1.32-34). Notice that Brutus stakes his whole honor on the truth of this claim: "Believe me for mine honour," he enjoins the plebs, "and have respect to mine honour, that you may believe" (3.2.14–16).

Some in Shakespeare's audience may balk here: "Really, Brutus? You say you loved Caesar. How do you figure that?" Marc Antony's brilliant follow-up seizes upon Brutus' appeal to honor, but uses it to sow seeds of skepticism in the audience: "He was my friend, faithful and just to me; / But Brutus says, he was ambitious," he adds, "and Brutus is an honourable man" (3.2.87–88). Indeed, after ten attestations that Brutus is "honourable," the plebs grow suspicious. (Methinks the politician doth protest too much?) Subtly and cunningly, Antony puts his finger on this seeming inconsistency:

> *I speak not to disprove what Brutus spoke,*
> *But here I am to speak what I do know.*
> *You all did love him once, not without cause:*
> *What cause withholds you then to mourn*
> *for him? (3.2.101–4)*

Would not a true friend of Caesar mourn the death of Caesar, even if that death were deemed necessary? Would not an honorable friend feel sorrow for that loss? Certainly, Brutus does not seem mournful when he urges the conspirators to greet the public with their hands, elbows, and swords bathed in Caesar's blood (3.1.107–11). But the man claims to love Caesar even as he slays him. How do we grapple with this apparent contradiction?

Before we write Brutus off as a liar, we must remember his golden virtues. Brutus is arguably the most selfless character in the play—a man who shows no concern for his own political career, image, or power, but thinks only about the common cause (5.5.69–73). Even when Cassius first reveals the assassination plot in act 1, scene 2, Brutus cuts him off at the pass, making plain his commitment to the noble:

If it be aught toward the general good,
Set honour in one eye, and death i'th' other,
And I will look on both indifferently.
For let the gods so speed me as I love
The name of honour more than I fear death. (1.2.85–89)

Notice that Brutus equates "honour" with "the general good." Cassius assures Brutus that "honour is the subject of [his] story," but in the monologue that follows, it becomes clear that "honor" means something very different to Cassius (1.2.92). Whereas Brutus equates honor with virtue, Cassius identifies it with public recognition (1.2.141–42). But Brutus remains driven by the higher meaning of "honor": "For my part," he confesses in soliloquy, "I know no personal cause to spurn at him / But for the general" (2.1.10–12).

The interesting psychological question then is not whether Brutus believed he loved Caesar, for there seems to be ample evidence that he did. Rather the perplexing puzzle is how he could believe it: i.e., according to what weird logic could loving Caesar and killing Caesar be reconciled? In what strange psychology could such words and deeds prove compatible?

For one thing, it's important to note that Brutus kills Caesar not because the latter embodies an actual tyrant, but only because he represents a potential tyrant. "'Tis a common proof," Brutus judges,

> *That lowliness is young ambition's ladder*
> *Whereto the climber upward turns his face;*
> *But when he once attains the upmost round*
> *He then unto the ladder turns his back,*
> *Looks in the clouds, scorning the base degrees*
> *By which he did ascend. So Caesar may.*
> *Then, lest he may, prevent. (2.1.21–28)*

Blurring the conditional and the indicative, Brutus concludes that because Caesar "may" climb the ladder of ambition Caesar "must" be prevented. Of course, what's conspicuously absent from these reflections is any deep consideration of Caesar's real character. In fact, Brutus explicitly grounds his whole argument upon Caesar's yet unrealized ambition ("He would be crowned: How that might change his nature, there's the question" [2.1.12–13]). Brutus loves the real Caesar. What he opposes is the hypothetical threat. This psychological distinction may explain how Brutus could kill Caesar and love him at the same time: In a way, the assassination in act 3, scene 1 isn't about the real Caesar at all. It's about the unhatched adder—the potential despot, the possible worm.

Of course, that thinking contains deep flaws. If we define "imprudence" as the culpable failure to apply good principles to right action, then Brutus here clearly manifests the political form of that vice. The problem isn't that he lacks good values (honor, nobility, the cause of the common good). Rather, the issue is one of judgment. Consumed by the mere thought of Caesar's dark ascendancy, Brutus overlooks the real political circumstances—in this case, Caesar himself, the man, the individual with his unique contours of character. And isn't it always the circumstances, not just the principles, that one must consider in government? For as Edmund Burke so astutely noted,

> *Circumstances (which with some gentlemen pass for nothing) give in reality to every political principle its distinguishing colour, and discriminating effect. The circumstances are what render every civil and political scheme beneficial or noxious to mankind.*[1]

The story of Brutus teaches us to attend to the "colour" and "effect" of politics because the conditions of decision-making matter. And Shakespeare shows us what goes wrong if we fail to exercise our ideals with prudence.

Sadly, Brutus realizes his error only at the end of the play—the moment of his suicide. "Caesar, now be still," Brutus pleads as he falls on his sword. "I killed not thee with half so good a will" (5.5.51–52). Here particular and personal justice wins out over big-picture political aims. Whereas the first death of the play (the regicide) aimed to satisfy the many, the last death (his suicide) comes for the justice of one—Caesar himself.

Brutus tried to love Caesar. Brutus tried to love Rome. But he didn't understand the relationship between these two loves, how the love of Caesar and the love of Rome were inextricably bound up in one another.

CHAPTER NINE

THE TEMPEST AND THE LIMITS OF LITERATURE

Poetry is neither religion, nor social engineering.

Allen Tate, *On the Limits of Poetry*

While any one Shakespeare play sometimes suffers a variety of flaky readings, *The Tempest* may be the play most susceptible to the mystical variety of silliness. It has entertained a strange range of symbolic interpretations, some seeing the play as a parable for the tripartite soul, others as a proto-Nietzschean myth of power, and still others as a dramatic form of gnostic religion. In the words of Frank Kermode, with *The Tempest*, we go "whoring after strange gods of allegory."[1]

G. K. Chesterton discerned a helpful approach to symbolism in this play. The question with *The Tempest*, he said, is not whether Shakespeare uses symbols, but what kind:

Shakespeare was a symbolist of the genuine type. . . . A

real symbol of a certain law is not a mere cipher-term arbitrarily connected with that law, but an example of that law. A plough is symbol of the toil of all things because it is an instance of it. The parables of the New Testament, for instance, are built wholly upon this principle; so are the one or two mystical plays of Shakespeare.[2]

Ariel may come to stand for the imagination in some sense, but the character is not a code or "cipher-term," as a red traffic light is an arbitrary cipher for "STOP." In carrying out the edicts of Prospero's imaginative project, Ariel exemplifies the productive, invisible, shaping power of that deeply human faculty. *The Tempest* is full of this kind of symbolism. It figures its meaning illustratively, not cryptically, through the desires and actions of characters.

In this qualified sense of the word "symbolism," then, it is worth thinking about Prospero as a symbolic portrait of the poetic imagination—both its powers and its limits. Of course, I am not the first to make this association between Prospero and poetry, and one might draw up elaborate theories about deeper biographical connections to Shakespeare. But I don't think we have to resort to that kind of conjectural thought to link Prospero to literary art. Rather, following Chesterton's example, we can confidently say that Prospero is a symbol for the poetic imagination simply because he is an example of poetic imagination. Throughout *The Tempest*, Prospero seeks to teach, to move, and in some cases even to delight other characters through conjurations, image-making, and the shaping of "vanities" (4.1.41). As Dona Gower puts it, he uses his powers "for putting his pupils in touch with reality through imagination, through . . . poiesis."[3] Prospero's magic, in other words, is not merely phantasma; it is a revelation of things—of the spiritual landscape and moral interior.

There are two ways in which Prospero embodies poetic thought. First, he offers his enemies what we might call experiential education as he uses his magical powers to give Antonio and company a taste of his own past trials. In act 1, scene 2, as father and daughter watch the magical storm from the safety of the shore, Prospero asks his daughter, Miranda, to imagine the scene of their escape from Milan, the day when their comrades snuck them out into the stormy sea:

> *There they hoist us,*
> *To cry to th' sea, that roar'd to us; to sigh*
> *To th' winds, whose pity, sighing back again,*
> *Did us but loving wrong. (1.2.148–51)*

In that initial voyage, only the "sighing" elements seemed to sympathize. Now Prospero makes his subjects experience fear and desertion because he himself experienced that fear and desertion. He aims, as Elizabeth Spiller writes, "to make his enemies know what he has known."[4] In this respect, Prospero is a teacher, not only through books, but also through images. By conjured forms, he offers an experiential mode of knowledge not unlike the poet's: Just as a Milton gives his readers a glimpse of the world-distorting psychology of sin, just as a Sophocles flashes before us the terrors of true self-knowledge, so Prospero escorts his subjects through the dark consequences of their lust for power. He offers them moral knowledge through experience.

Second, Prospero embodies the poetic imagination by teaching through wonder. The clearest moment of this craft transpires in act 4, scene 1 with the wedding masque. True to the form of the English wedding-masque, the mage weaves the couple into the story, providing a dramatic representation of faithful, married happiness. With Venus and Cupid's threats deflected, the couple's purity unlocks the blessings of the gods, and Heaven may now descend to "sport" with earth, as Iris, whose "wat'ry arch" binds sky and earth, figures forth the blessings that accompany fidelity. By his beautiful "vanity," Prospero aims to reinforce an idea of the goodness of marriage in the minds of Ferdinand and Miranda through an education of images. Before, he communicated the importance of that goodness through an injunction, but in this scene he transmits the good of that ideal through pictures. The masque is a mimesis, an artistic imitation, which both teaches and delights, capturing the affections, enticing a sense of wonder for goodness itself.

Wonder, we notice, forms an important motif in Shakespeare's play. Miranda's name comes from *mirare*, meaning "to wonder or marvel at" (hence Ferdinand's "Admir'd Miranda" line in act 3, scene 1). We remember her famous lines at discovering the newcomers on the island: "O wonder! /

How many goodly creatures are there here! / How beauteous mankind is! O brave new world / That has such people in't!" (5.1.181–84). Ferdinand marvels at Miranda as well: "O you wonder!" (1.2.427). Gonzalo calls their salvation from the tempest a "miracle" and names the island a place of "wonder" and "amazement" (5.1.104–5). Through wonder, the human soul arrives at the threshold of new wisdom. As Socrates claims in the *Theaetetus*, "Wondering: this is where philosophy begins and nowhere else."[5]

But Prospero also embodies the limits of poetry by showing us something his magic can't accomplish, something his images can't conquer. The reader may remember how just when the revelry of Prospero's masque reaches its peak the illusion comes to a chaotic halt. Here the mage remembers the conspiracy of Caliban and his confederates and offers a strange, meditative speech on the insubstantiality and ephemerality of his magic:

> Our revels now are ended. These our actors
> (As I foretold you) were all spirits, and
> Are melted into air, into thin air,
> And like the baseless fabric of this vision,
> The cloud-capp'd tow'rs, the gorgeous palaces,
> The solemn temples, the great globe itself,
> Yea, all which it inherit, shall dissolve,
> And like this insubstantial pageant faded
> Leave not a rack behind. We are such stuff
> As dreams are made on; and our little life

Is rounded with a sleep. (4.1.146–58)

Prospero's "revels" figure a beautiful reality. But the "revels" themselves are only "baseless fabric" and "cloud-capp'd towers." That is to say, they have no intrinsic power to change people who don't want to be changed. Ferdinand and Miranda may be captivated by the glory of the masque, and they may be moved by its lively picture of goodness, but Prospero's antagonists are still out to get him. With his magic books, he is at best a conjurer of images, and without his books, Caliban says, he is "but a sot" (3.2.93). When the poet's "charms are all o'erthrown," his remaining strength is, to quote the epilogue, "most faint" (5.ep.1.3).

Allen Tate once noted that "poetry is neither religion, nor social engineering"—meaning, I think, that the human imagination (for all its glory) grants neither heavenly grace nor earthly dominion.[6] Poetry has neither the transformative power of religion nor the coercive power of politics. In a way, Prospero discovers these limits at the end of the play as his powers peter out, and perhaps this discovery explains the thematic turn toward Christian charity in the final act. Once the mage's "project" is finally complete, Ariel arrives to tell Prospero that all is as he has planned it. The king and his retinue are all trapped in a grove by Prospero's cell. Of all these miserable characters, Gonzalo is the most pitiable:

His tears run down his beard like winter's drops
From eaves of reeds. Your charm so strongly works 'em

> That if you now beheld them, your affections
> Would become tender.
>
> PROSPERO. Dost thou think so, spirit?
>
> ARIEL. Mine would sir, were I human.
>
> PROSPERO. And mine shall.
> Hast thou, which art but air, a touch, a feeling
> Of their afflictions, and shall not myself,
> One of their kind, that relish all as sharply
> Passion as they, be kindlier mov'd than thou art?
> Though with their high wrongs I am strook to th' quick,
> Yet, with my nobler reason, 'gainst my fury
> Do I take part. The rarer action is
> In virtue than in vengeance. They being penitent,
> The sole drift of my purpose doth extend
> Not a frown further. (5.1.16–30)

Up to this point, we've been looking at Prospero as the teacher. Interestingly, we now see him as the student. At the height of his "project," he gains an unexpected pity for the king and his men. But how does he gain it? Through the imagination, it seems. Through a feeling apprehension of his enemies' pitiable state. Shakespeare's audience knows for a fact that Ariel's vivid sketch of Gonzalo stirs this compassion in Prospero's soul because the tears mentioned in lines 16–17 are mentioned again by Prospero at the scene of reconciliation, lines 62–64. So through an act of imaginative identification, of "nobler reason," Prospero finds the ability to show mercy, and by "feeling . . . [his enemies'] afflictions," he can forgive their evil, checking his anger with the "rarer action" of pardon.

Yes, poetry is weak. But it is enough. These final scenes from *The Tempest* show us the limits of literature, yet they also show us how the imagination can still guide the soul toward good action: to seek reconciliation, to offer pardon. Indeed, one can only face life by living it. At the end of the play, Prospero again must take up his dukedom; the nymphs must leave Ferdinand and Miranda to work out the challenging realities that attend marriage, and this means reentering a life of hardship and pain. But when this transition is made by "nobler reason"—that is, when the soul can, like Prospero, join the rational and imaginative faculties in an act of sympathy—the soul can forgive the world. It can even forgive a Caliban. Poesis is married to mercy.

Perhaps that's the best thing we can say about literature: It is spiritually propaedeutic. Literature is not itself grace, but somehow it prepares us for grace. For those like Miranda who can marvel at the broken world and still acknowledge its "brave" and "beauteous" glory, who can join others in sympathetic imagination ("O! I have suffered / With those that I saw suffer"), there will still be a place for poetry (1.2.5–6). It was necessary that Prospero "drown" his book for true forgiveness to take place. But we remember that Prospero's move to mercy is inspired by beauty. Shining instances of beauty will always inspire mercy.

APPENDIX

FIVE STRATEGIES FOR STICKING WITH SHAKESPEARE

I never quite despair and I read Shakspeare.

John Keats,
Letter to Benjamin Robert Haydon

At the beginning of this book, I mentioned a few august figures who made a regular habit of reading the Bard. Now in closing, I will sketch out a few practicable strategies for doing the same. Naturally, I want to avoid outlining anything too programmatic here. My aim throughout has been to make space for literary meditation, and true *meditatio* always resists the mechanical. Still, everyone must start somewhere with the Shakespeare life, so perhaps it is worth considering a few specific ways to move forward.

A quick point of clarification: No one should feel obliged to adopt this entire list of strategies at one time (talk about a burden). Instead, I recommend picking one or two and trying them out for a spell. See how it goes. The great American poet John Berryman may have thought it "awfully silly . . . to do anything but read Shakespeare," but most of us, I suspect, believe otherwise.[1] We want to leave room for other activities, not to mention other great authors—Milton, Austen, Auden, and so forth. Approach Shakespeare then not as another "reading list," but as one good part of a larger good life.

With that more modest goal in mind, let me offer this non-exhaustive list of five ways to stick with Shakespeare:

LISTEN

In my experience, it is very difficult to find time outside school to watch film productions of Shakespeare's work. Audio is another story. Film demands a sedentary spectator, but the audiobook liberates the listener to do other things while soaking in the story: driving, jogging, folding laundry, or even cooking. When you adopt this listening approach, it is surprising how much Shakespeare you can enjoy within the parameters of your ordinary schedule. If you have a fifteen-minute commute to work, you can finish Macbeth in just one workweek. The podcasts can wait.

The gold standard for Shakespeare audio is still the Complete Arkangel Shakespeare: a magisterial, unabridged collection of thirty-eight plays, peerless in their production quality, replete with vocal talents like David Tennant, Richard Griffiths, and Sophie Thompson. You may also wish to take a look at the Folger Shakespeare Library and Naxos Library recordings or find some decent freebies on Librivox—a deep archive of public domain audiobooks.

HOST A SHAKESPEARE PARTY

"The verbal texture of Shakespeare," Nabokov once said, "is the greatest the world has known."[2] Implication: Something magical happens when we hear the text instead of merely sub-vocalizing the words in private reading. Why not stage a reading at your home, accompanied by good food and drink? Granted, a brisk trip through *Coriolanus* or *Anthony and Cleopatra* in one evening is no cakewalk, and the first few scenes may seem arduous. But the joy increases as you go along. Why not gather some friends, prepare some vittles, and give it a shot?

MEMORIZE

Recently my theater colleague at Grove City College had the fun idea of filming several Shakespeare scenes across campus, and much to my initial dismay, she asked me to perform King Henry's "St. Crispin's Day Speech." At first, I blanched at the thought of committing fifty lines to memory, and the stress of the impending performance actually made me feel ill. But after the preliminary panic subsided, I made a modest goal for myself: five lines a day for ten days.

In retrospect, I am not sure that I played a very good Harry, but I will say that the speech gave me a new outlook on Shakespeare memorization: Now I see the thing can be done. At present, my mental shelves lie fairly bare of Shakespeare, but when I am old, I hope to be like Lionel Logue from *The King's Speech* (2010) or John Keating from *Dead Poet's Society* (1989). I hope to have a mind stuffed with shimmering lines—crammed like a stocked pantry with the Bard's dazzling analogies, quick quips, and somber soliloquies. The question for Shakespeare fans is not whether it can be done, but how.

For those of us with kids, the best plan may be to learn this stuff as they do. Ken Ludwig's *How to Teach Your Children Shakespeare* (2013) is an excellent resource, as is Charles and Mary Lamb's *Tales from Shakespeare* (1807). Pair the passages in Ludwig with the prose retellings in Lamb and you have yourself a great children's curriculum for Shakespeare memorization.

DEDICATE YOURSELF TO A PLAY

Eventually, you may come to discover that one or more plays stand out from the rest of the canon. Some particular piece speaks to your core. Maybe that work for you is *Hamlet*. Maybe it's the entire Henriad. For whatever reason, *As You Like It* chose me. I find that that play perpetually rewards many rereadings.

In his little book on literature and the Christian faith, *Poetry as a Means of Grace* (1941), Charles Grosvenor Osgood wrote a delightful chapter called "Your Poet"—a graceful defense of imaginative reading which puts forward the enchanting idea that all serious readers should disciple themselves under a single great literary author.[3] I would like to emend Osgood's idea only slightly for Shakespeare: In addition to finding "Your Poet," find "Your Play." Find the work that you want to know backward and forward, inside and out. Ideally this process happens "less by deliberate selection than by natural congruence."[4] But however it happens, stick with it and see what emerges from that long-term friendship.

READ SHAKESPEARE IN A YEAR

This option is by far the most ambitious track of the five. I do not recommend it for everyone, and I certainly do not recommend it as an indefinite life commitment. That said, "Shakespeare-in-a-Year" may be the adventure for you at some point. Most summers, a quiet week in Cape Cod or Key West sounds like the ideal vacation. But at some point, every family toys with the idea of a cross-country camping expedition.

For many, tackling this body of work in one calendar year looks daunting. ("Do you mean I am supposed to add this to my already failing devotional life?" asks the bleary-eyed father of five.) In fact, the feat in question may prove less Herculean than we originally suppose. One can break down the big goal into a manageable schedule in a couple different ways. Take the "clean average" approach. Line totals for Shakespeare vary from edition to edition, but a ballpark sum for the whole canon lies somewhere around 114,500 lines, which means that an abstemious reader averaging 350 lines a day not only finishes the plays in a year, but also leaves room for almost a month of off-time. Another way to pace yourself is the "work a week" strategy: thirty-nine plays + six poetic works = forty-five weeks of reading. That's seven weeks left for catchup and vacation.

Whatever way you divide up the journey, avoid marching your way straight through the canon in laundry-list fashion. Try to include some highpoints and holidays in your schedule. A Shakespeare reading-plan isn't something sacred like a church calendar. Still, there ought to be a quasi-liturgical logic to the thing. Most of Shakespeare is a moveable feast, but in my own opinion, there are a few fixed fêtes for the Shakespeare year:

1. *Twelfth Night* at Christmas/Epiphany
2. *As You Like It* in Lent
3. *Julius Caesar* on the Ides of March (March 15th)
4. *The Winter's Tale* at Easter
5. *A Midsummer Night's Dream* near midsummer
6. *Henry V* near October 25th (the Battle of Agincourt)
7. *The Tempest* during Advent

Plays 1, 3, 5, and 6 take place during the time indicated, and plays 2, 4, and 7 have strong thematic ties. (I also find it interesting that 2 and 7 were first performed near Lent and Advent, respectively.) The Folger Library website offers similar ideas for pairing Shakespeare with the seasons.[6] You might want to use their resources as another template.

These are just some ideas to get you going. Whatever you settle with, remember that the goal is not a checklist of accomplishments, but a life enhanced by a beloved author. Ultimately, we read his plays for more than historical knowledge and cultural literacy. We also read them to meditate on their wisdom. He is, as Coleridge taught us, an "inexhaustible mine."

Many writers will bless your life. Shakespeare is one of them. Perhaps his complex yet resplendent image of the world will help you see some of the "good in every thing." Perhaps, in the hours of your own meditation, Shakespeare will speak to you.

NOTES

All Shakespeare citations come from The Riverside Shakespeare, 2nd ed.

INTRODUCTION

1. See especially Basil's letter "To Young Men, on How They Might Derive Profit from Pagan Literature" for a rich exploration of this idea.
2. John Calvin, *Institutes of the Christian Religion*, vol. 1, trans. Ford Lewis Battles (Philadelphia: Westminster, 1960), 273.
3. David V. Hicks, *Norms & Nobility: A Treatise on Education* (New York: University Press of America, 1999), 98.
4. Hugh of St. Victor, *The Didascalicon* (New York: Columbia University Press, 1991), 93.
5. Francis Bacon, "Of Studies," in *Bacon's Essays*, ed. Richard Whatley (London: Parker, 1858), 474.
6. Samuel Taylor Coleridge, "The Drama Generally, and Public Taste," in *Shakespeare, Ben Jonson, Beaumont and Fletcher: Notes and Lectures* (Liverpool: E. Howell, 1881), 40–41.

CHAPTER ONE
HAMLET AND WHAT MOVES US

1. John Senior, "Personal Interview," quoted in James Taylor, *Poetic Knowledge: The Recovery of Education* (Albany: SUNY Press, 1998), 82.
2. Charlotte Mason, *A Philosophy of Education* (Middletown: Living Book, 2017), 18.
3. Josef Pieper, F*aith, Hope, Love* (San Francisco: Ignatius, 1997), 43.

CHAPTER TWO
THREE UNOFFENSIVE THEMES IN THE TAMING OF THE SHREW

1. W. H. Auden, "The Taming of the Shrew, King John, and Richard II," in *Lectures on Shakespeare*, ed. Arthur Kirsch (Princeton: Princeton University Press, 2002), 63–64.
2. Coppélia Kahn, "'The Taming of the Shrew': Shakespeare's Mirror of Marriage," Modern Language Studies 5 (1975) 88.
3. Anne Barton, "The Taming of the Shrew," in *The Riverside Shakespeare*, ed. G. Blakemore Evans and J. J. M. Tobin (Boston: Houghton-Mifflin, 1997), 138.
4. Auden, "The Taming of the Shrew, King John, and Richard II," 63.
5. Russell A. Fraser, *Shakespeare's Poetics: In Relation to King Lear* (Abingdon: Routledge, 2005), 150.
6. I have in mind here those works ancient and modern that share the antique idea of the will as a mediating power be-

tween reason and appetite: e.g., the famous chariot allegory from Plato's *Phaedrus* (246a–54e) or the "Men without Chests" chapter in C. S. Lewis' *The Abolition of Man*.

7. Brian Morris, "The Themes of Education and Metamorphosis Unify the Play," in Readings on The Taming of the Shrew, ed. Laura Marvel (San Diego: Greenhaven, 2000), 77.

8. Alvin B. Kernan, "The Transforming Power of Plays and Play-Acting," in *Readings on The Taming of the Shrew*, ed. Laura Marvel (San Diego: Greenhaven, 2000), 83.

9. Trevor McNeely, *Proteus Unmasked: Sixteenth-Century Rhetoric and the Art of Shakespeare* (Cranbury: Associated University Press, 2004), 142–43.

10. Peter Saccio, "Shrewd and Kindly Farce," Shakespeare Survey 37.1 (1984) 36.

11. See, for instance, Lynda Boose, "The Taming of the Shrew, Good Husbandry, and Enclosure," in *Shakespeare Reread: The Texts in New Contexts*, ed. Russ McDonald (Ithaca: Cornell University Press, 1994), 195.

CHAPTER THREE
A THOUSAND SEVERAL TONGUES

1. Juvenal, "Satire XIII," in *Juvenal and Persius*, trans. G. G. Ramsay (London: Heineman, 1918), 261.

2. Saint Augustine, *Confessions*, trans. Henry Chadwick (Oxford: Oxford University Press, 1998), 150.

3. Agnes Heller, *The Time Is Out of Joint: Shakespeare as Philosopher of History* (Lanham: Rowman & Littlefield, 2002), 277.

4. Thomas Hobbes, *Leviathan* (New York: Penguin, 1982) 2.29.
5. Adam Smith, *The Theory of Moral Sentiments* (Cambridge: Cambridge University Press, 2002), 6.3.
6. A chilling passage to this effect is found in Hegel's *The Philosophy of History* (Mineola: Dover, 2004), 56.
7. Robert Vischer, *Conscience and the Common Good: Reclaiming the Space between Person and State* (Cambridge: Cambridge University Press, 2010), 72.

CHAPTER FOUR
THE CONVERSE OF BREATH

1. Emma Smith, "Love's Labour's Lost," *Approaching Shakespeare* (podcast), May 27, 2015, accessed October 16, 2020, https://podcasts.ox.ac.uk/loves-labours-lost/.
Matt. 5:37
2. Roger Scruton, *Fools, Frauds and Firebrands: Thinkers of the New Left* (London: Bloomsbury, 2015), 160.
3. Louis Althusser, *For Marx*, trans. Ben Brewster (London: Verso, 2005), 209.

CHAPTER FIVE
MIDSUMMER:
A CASE STUDY IN POETIC IMAGINATION

1. A. W. Schlegel, "Lecture XXIV," in *Lectures on Dramatic Art and Literature*, trans. John Black, rev. ed. (London: George Bell, 1894), 393.

NOTES

2. Samuel Pepys, *The Diary of Samuel Pepys* (London: Macmillan, 1905), 151.
3. Malcolm Guite, *Faith, Hope and Poetry: Theology and the Poetic Imagination* (New York: Ashgate, 2008), 54–66.
4. Guite, *Faith, Hope and Poetry*, 62.
5. Stephen Greenblatt, *Shakespeare's Freedom* (Chicago: Chicago University Press, 2010), 116–17.
6. Phillip Sidney, "The Defense of Poesy" in *Sir Philip Sidney: Selected Writings*, ed. Richard Dutton (New York: Routledge, 2002), 108.
7. Sidney, "The Defense of Poesy," 113–14.
8. Sidney, "The Defense of Poesy," 121.
9. Archibald MacLeish, "Ars Poetica," in *Collected Poems, 1917–1982* (Boston: Houghton-Mifflin, 1985), 106–7.
10. C. S. Lewis, *Poetry and Prose in the Sixteenth Century* (Oxford: Clarendon, 1990), 61.
11. Brian Vickers, "Introduction," in *English Renaissance Literary Criticism*, ed. Brian Vickers (Oxford: Oxford University Press, 1999), 53.

CHAPTER SIX
HENRY V AND THE
SHRUGGING SHAKESPEARE

1. William Hazlitt, *Characters of Shakespeare's Plays* (London: Templeman, 1854), 205.
2. W. H. Auden, "The Taming of the Shrew, King John, and Richard II," in *Lectures on Shakespeare*, ed. Arthur Kirsch (Princeton: Princeton University Press, 2002), 64.

3. Norman Rabkin, "Rabbits, Ducks, and Henry V," *Shakespeare Quarterly* 28.3 (Summer 1977) 279.
4. A. D. Nutall, *Shakespeare, The Thinker* (New Haven: Yale University Press, 2007), 1.
5. Harold Bloom, *Shakespeare: The Invention of the Human* (New York: Riverhead, 1980), 14–15.
6. Edmund Burke, *Reflections on the Revolution in France*, ed. J. G. A. Pocock (Indianapolis: Hackett, 1987), 67.7,
7. Marjorie Garber, *Shakespeare After All* (New York: Anchor, 2004), 3.
8. Gustave Flaubert, *The Letters of Gustave Flaubert: 1830–1857*, ed. Francis Steegmuller (Cambridge: Harvard University Press, 1980), 86.
9. Wayne Booth, *The Rhetoric of Fiction*, rev. ed. (Chicago: Chicago University Press, 2012), 75–76.
10. Booth, *The Rhetoric of Fiction*, 78.
11. Booth, *The Rhetoric of Fiction*, 387.
12. Glenn Arbery, *Why Literature Matters: Permanence and the Politics of Reputation* (Wilmington: ISI, 2001), 229–30.

CHAPTER SEVEN
THE WONDER OF ARDEN

1. C. S. Lewis, "On Stories," in *On Stories: And Other Essays on Literature* (New York: Harcourt, 1982), 7.
2. Stanley Wells, *Shakespeare: A Life in Drama* (New York: Norton, 1995), 170.
3. Hannibal Hamlin, *The Bible in Shakespeare* (Oxford: Oxford University Press, 2013), 152.

4. Some of Pieper's best treatments of this subject can be found in *Leisure: The Basis of Culture, Happiness and Contemplation*, and *In Tune with the World: A Theory of Festivity*.
5. Marjorie Garber, "The Education of Orlando," in Bloom's *Modern Critical Interpretations: William Shakespeare's "As You Like It,"* ed. Harold Bloom (New York: Chelsea, 2004), 61.
6. Garber, "The Education of Orlando," 71.
7. John Senior and Dennis B. Quinn, "Job," tape 4 (Casper: Powder River Literary Society, 1990).
8. Robert Lloyd, "Shakespeare: An Epistle to David Garrick," in *The Familiar Poems of Robert Lloyd* (London: Longman, 1805), 26.

CHAPTER EIGHT
HOW COULD BRUTUS LOVE CAESAR?

1. Burke, *Reflections on the Revolution in France*, ed. J. G. A. Pocock (Indianapolis: Hackett, 1987), 7.

CHAPTER NINE
THE TEMPEST AND THE LIMITS OF LITERATURE

1. Frank Kermode, "Introduction," in *The Tempest*, ed. Frank Kermode (New York: Methuen, 1964), lxxx.
2. G. K. Chesterton, *The Soul of Wit: G. K. Chesterton on William Shakespeare* (Mineola: Dover, 2012), 232.
3. Dona Gower, "The Tempest and Paideia," in *Classic Texts and the Nature of Authority*, ed. Donald and Louise Cowan (Dallas: Dallas Institute, 1993), 247.

4. Elizabeth Spiller, "Shakespeare and the Making of Early Modern Science: Resituating Prospero's Art," South Central Review 26.1–2 (2009) 25–26.
5. Plato, *Theaetetus*, trans. M. J. Levett (Indianapolis: Hackett, 1992), 19.
6. Allen Tate, "Introduction," in *On the Limits of Poetry: Selected Essays, 1928–1948* (Santa Clarita: Books for Libraries, 1970), xi.

APPENDIX
FIVE STRATEGIES FOR STICKING WITH SHAKESPEARE

1. John Berryman, quoted in Anne Barton, "John Berryman's Flying Horse," *The New York Review*, September 23, 1999, https://www.nybooks.com/articles/1999/09/23/john-berrymans-flying-horse/.
2. Vladimir Nabokov, quoted in Sam Schuman, *Nabokov's Shakespeare* (New York: Bloomsbury, 2014), x.
3. Incidentally, Osgood has his reservations about choosing Shakespeare as one's poet—not because Shakespeare isn't a great playwright, but because he believes Shakespeare lacks a certain kind of moral clarity. I wrestled with this kind of concern in the sixth meditation.
4. Charles Osgood, *Poetry as a Means of Grace* (Princeton: Princeton University Press, 1941), 22.
5. These composition dates come from *The Oxford Shakespeare: The Complete Works*, 2nd. ed.
6. Ian Doescher, "The Shakespeare 2020 Project: A Plan to

NOTES

Read Through the Complete Works in One Year," Folger Shakespeare Library, https://shakespeareandbeyond.folger.edu/2019/12/06/shakespeare-2020-project-reading-plan-complete-works-one-year/.

ACKNOWLEDGMENTS

First, my heartfelt thanks goes to my colleague and friend Christopher Franklin for reading through many drafts and helping me discern the vision of this book. So much of my thinking on literature and the pursuit of wisdom I owe to you. Long live the conversations which forged this text! I am also indebted to my colleagues in the English Department at Grove City College for their constancy and friendship and to my brilliant mentors at the University of Dallas, who taught me much of what I know about reading Shakespeare: Scott Crider, Robert Dupree, and Andrew Moran. I carry your teaching with me.

On a more personal note, I mention the gift of my children—Ezra, Silas, Ainley, and Zoe Claire—whose love of good stories always encourages me to teach Shakespeare for the things that matter. Thank you for regularly reminding me of literature's power with your admirable and unaffected love of story. I am also grateful for my parents, Walter and Patricia Mayo, whose love and encouragement in things beautiful and good forms a living backdrop to these pages.

Finally, my wife: Where would this book be if not for you, Bethany? You gave me the encouragement; you gave me the time to think and write. More, you were my friend in stories and ideas. This is for you.

ABOUT THE PUBLISHER

The CiRCE Institute is a non-profit 501(c)3 organization that exists to promote and support classical education in the school and in the home. We seek to identify the ancient principles of learning, to communicate them enthusiastically, and to apply them vigorously in today's educational settings through curricula development, teacher and parent training, events, multimedia resources, and book publishing.

Learn more at www.circeinstitute.com or on social media.